A CLASSICAL
YOUTH

A CLASSICAL YOUTH

and other pieces

MICHAEL LONGSON

I have to express my indebtedness to *Punch* for their permission
to reproduce the verses on pages 117 to 134.

Frontispiece: Portrait of the author in his youth.

First published in Great Britain in 1985 by Anthony Blond

Anthony Blond is an imprint of Muller, Blond & White Limited,
55/57 Great Ormond Street, London, WC1N 3HZ.

Copyright © 1985 Michael Longson

Poems pages 117 to 134 copyright © *Punch* 1933–1953

British Library Cataloguing in Publication Data

Longson, Michael
    A classical youth.
    1. Longson, Michael   2. Edinburgh Academy—
Biography   3. Classicists— Scotland—
Edinburgh—Biography   4. Teachers—Scotland—Edinburgh—Biography
I. Title
938'.007'12024   PA85.L7/

ISBN 0-85634-196-7

Printed and bound in Great Britain by
Redwood Burn Limited, Trowbridge, Wiltshire.

dedicated to John Tickner

CONTENTS

PROLOGUE

When I first conceived the idea of trying to write a book I turned for advice to my Wiser Self, an evasive person who is seldom there when he is wanted and in my view has never made quite the contribution he might have made to our partnership — not, that is, if the evidence of his first seventy-odd years on the job is anything to go by.

This time he was more available than usual, and he listened without the contempt I had expected when I told him that some thirty years had passed since the arrival of Malcolm Muggeridge and his new policies in Bouverie Street had cut short my career as a versifier for *Punch,* and that I rather wanted to publish something else before I went hence and was no more seen.

The ensuing dialogue between my Wiser Self and my Ordinary Self went roughly as follows — thus or somewhat thus, as the splendid A.W. Verrall puts it.

W.S: 'Yes, I can understand your feeling like that. But what do you propose to write *about?* You haven't gone deeply enough into any classical subject to attempt an academic thesis, and you have nothing of what it takes to do a novel. I repeat, what are you going to write *about?'*

O.S: 'I've debated that question a lot, W.S., and the only thing I can think of is my ... my ... well, my life, W.S.'

W.S: '*Your life?* And what has *your life* to offer that other people could conceivably want to read about it? You're a me-type, you must admit, not an I-type: you don't do things, they just happen to you.'

O.S: 'Yes, of course I admit that, W.S. But some of the things that have happened to me have been quite interesting, you know. I think I might be able to make something of them.'

W.S: 'All right, you can't do much harm, I suppose. But we must be practical. You realise, I hope, that this precious life of yours will have to end at twenty-three.'

O.S: 'Eh?'

1

W.S: 'It stands to reason. You're on safe enough ground with your days as a schoolboy or undergraduate; but after that the farther your story went on the harder the going would be. A classical schoolmaster's ideas of what is important aren't universally shared, you know; your ingenious scholastic theories, all the ripe wisdom accumulated over many long years — they wouldn't be very enthralling to most people. And there would be dangers as well. Bit by bit you would find yourself more and more bound to write, sometimes critically and in detail, about people who are still alive and can still read. You would worry yourself sick over who must be brought in and who needn't, and how much you ought to say about whom, with a high probability of making a mess of it in the end. Do you see my point?'

O.S: 'Yes, W.S. I see it very well.'

W.S: 'Good. We are agreed then on the ending; it remains to consider the beginning. "It was on April 17th in 1911 that I first saw the light of day:" we can't risk anything of that kind. In fact, since you admit that even you can't work up much enthusiasm about your early childhood, and since the lyrical evocation of a vanished age isn't quite in your line, the less you have to say about that period the better. So out go the green fields and the little brook with frogs in it, and out go with them all the loving or less loving relations — yes, even the Aunt Molly who was always so kind to you on your long leaves from school. All you need tell your hypothetical readers is that your father was a Manchester barrister who captained a good Cheshire cricket club for twenty-five years and eventually became a well-regarded County Court judge in Derbyshire; that you had a sister called Ruth who was two years your elder; that in your first few years you were under the tutelage of Mamie Sewell, whose little monkey face and funny buzzy voice gave Ruth and you a deep sense of utter security that neither of you were ever to know since; that you can still never read the sestet of Wilfred Owen's "What passing bells" without thinking of a glorious morning in the June of 1916, when you went up to the nursery after breakfast to find your beautiful Mabel Ashley crying her heart out with an opened letter in front of her; that you always accepted quite equably the fact that in many ways you were more stupid than other children, even when you knew you were considered to be rather good at your books, and even when you were already developing the mild megalomania which led you at seven or eight to announce your intention of being buried with great pomp and ceremony. You can tell them all that if you will. But then for goodness' sake get on to the one theme you can write about with some pretence to authority — school.'

2

BOWDON AND HALE

Culcheth Hall School for Girls (Boys Admitted in the Kindergarten) was founded by the Misses Lang at some time back in the nineteenth century — far enought to have been attended by my mother and at least two of her sisters as well, so that Ruth and I were technically known as 'grandchildren'. It presumably started as a large Victorian house with a spacious lawn in front of it sloping down to the main road; but by our day there were other important buildings too, and a well-kept upper lawn surrounded by trees, and a playground and tennis-courts and a big playing-field across the side road. The school was still run by the Misses Lang, or rather, so far as the world could see, it was run by Miss Edith, a vigorous grey-haired woman with a florid complexion and keen but benevolent brown eyes. From the long prosperity of her reign it was clear that she was a highly capable headmistress, but she had also a dangerous sentimental side which the Culcheth motto fatally reflected: even for a girls' school 'Looking upwards like the daisies' was not quite good enough. She was often silently accompanied by Miss Mary, who would walk beside her a foot or so behind. To Miss Mary we accorded the rather indeterminate respect due to the obviously junior partner; we none of us had any idea of what she actually did, but it is a fair guess that many of the hard administrative chores were hers to handle, and just conceivably she had a greater say in the decisions than she was ever given credit for. But somehow I can't see our Miss Mary as having been much of a grey eminence.

Most of my Culcheth memories are necessarily stray and haphazard: my silent aggrievement at the choosing of a *girl* in a class reconstruction to represent the prince who went down with the White Ship; the sudden deep blush on the face of a girl standing near me in a singing lesson, and my own sense of natural sympathy with her as the cause of her distress revealed itself in the pool forming on the floor between her feet; the ignominy of being continually pinched by a virago of a deskmate who was too vast

3

and too impenetrable of hide to be effectively pinched back; my last prize-giving, when I had the satisfaction of walking shyly back to my seat with my equal-top prize and afterwards stood on a bench in the cloak-room to kiss my favourite prefect good-bye. The favourite prefect was Peggy Neatby, already a friend of Ruth's and soon to become a friend of our whole family.

In Ruth's opinion the teaching at Culcheth wasn't particularly good, and since she had a two-years' start on me (we both first went there at six) and remained there for a further four years after I left, she obviously had much more evidence to go on than I. But it is my own experience that I must record, and my impressions were very much different from Ruth's. Whether I was ill- or well-taught in arithmetic I have no idea, for no congenitally bad mathematician can ever know which of those who tried to help him were as inefficient as they were on the face of it ineffective, and which did a wonderfully good job with highly unrewarding material. But I can speak with unqualified enthusiasm for the way in which I was taught history by Miss Craig, who awoke in me a love of the subject which none of her successors elsewhere was ever able to rearouse; and much the same could be said of the English teaching of Miss Eaton — though here a slight qualification should be added, one for which it would be unfair to blame Miss Eaton alone. For many years the tradition of English teaching in England suffered from a strange complaint which was apparently epidemic: in school on school throughout the country all the children seem to have been made to learn exactly the same poems, some of them poems of questionable literary merit, and rarely if ever was any explanation offered of what they were about. I can see now that old Kaspar was a little simple in the matter of great historic issues, but to this day I don't know what the good news was that they brought from Ghent to Aix.[1] Apart from that I can only say that I found all the reading I was given continuously stimulating and enriching: in my mind's eye, even now, it is at the far left-hand corner of the Culcheth upper lawn that the handsome and beloved young Baldur stands as he awaits the deadly mistletoe, it is through the Culcheth side-gate that the wooden horse is admitted and round one of the main Culcheth buildings that the desperate fighting goes on.

1. The junior forms at Culcheth were also introduced to a little masterpiece which deserved a wider recognition than it seems to have won:

> Pimpernel, Pimpernel, tell me true:
> What is the *weather* going to do?
> Will it be *wet,* or will it be *fine?*
> Will the *rain pour,* or will the *sun shine?*
> It's *no* use *asking* the *Lily* or *Rose:*
> *Only* the *dear* little *Pimpernel knows.*

I found a similar stimulation and enrichment in the singing classes led from the piano by the redoubtable Mrs. Soutar, and here again the memorable emphasis was on the traditional: 'The Raggle Taggle Gipsies, O' (what had the new-wedded lord done already to have been abandoned for so unpromising a crew?), 'Robin Adair', 'Jock o' Hazeldean', 'Barbara Allen', and my favourite of them all, of which I can supply neither the title nor even the first line, but the twig was on the branch and the branch was on the tree and the tree was in the wood and the green leaves grew all around around around and the green leaves grew all around. Every now and then, once a week perhaps, the juniors were also admitted to senior prayers, and it was through those short services that I first came to love Miller's Rockingham, long accepted as the perfect tune to 'When I survey the wondrous cross', but the time was 1917 or 1918, and for me the definitive last line will always be the fourfold refrain of the hymn to which we sang it then, 'Give peace, O God, give pe-e-eace again.'

Meanwhile there was that other half of life which had nothing to do with school.

One evening I sauntered down to the bottom of Vale Road and found Ruth at the stile leading to the field beyond, deep in talk with a girl I had never seen before. She was a pretty girl with a dusky face and gentle, dark eyes, and I thought, oh, she's nice, I do hope Ruth likes her. It turned out that Ruth did like her, and for several years Edie and her amenable cousin Johnny were our regular playmates. Their station was humbler than ours (the unhappy Edie had been virtually abandoned by her father at six after her mother's death, and was now living, with a much older and unsympathetic sister, in the cottage of her grandmother Mrs. Percival, a countrywoman of the great old Cheshire breed who was our charlady and my mother's most trusted confidante), so that as a matter of course all the playing was done either in our garden or in our house, and for every reason the leader in all our enterprises was Ruth. What form our outside games took I am wholly unable to remember, but there was one unforgettable indoor game for which our attic nursery with its big cupboard was just right, a variant of hide-and-seek called Rough Waters and Still Waters. Social distinction went almost for nothing, but Ruth and I had to let a little secret amusement temper our affection when Edie broke off our play with 'I must roon, or me gran'll shout', or when she looked in at the garden gate to announce, 'Can't come in now. Got to go Brooks's to get a loaf of bread for eat.'

This easy association with children of a quite different background came naturally to members of the Longson family, which

5

always lived a little apart from the conventional Bowdon, in its habits of thinking and behaving as in the local situation of its home. The other families we knew were as a rule also markedly more affluent than we; my mother had been brought up in the house of a rich man, but she was the only one of the five sisters to marry a comparatively poor one. I have never understood why my father made so little money. That he was far from untalented is shown clearly enough by the liberal use that C.P. Scott's *Manchester Guardian* made of his early free-lance writings, including a weekly column on golf which ran for ten years and long afterwards was compared by Neville Cardus to the work of Bernard Darwin himself; and he is unlikely to have been stupid or incompetent at his profession. A private theory of mine, which may be only a projection of my own weakness, is that he shrank from the responsibilities involved by the more lucrative cases. True, he accepted a County Court judgeship in 1931, but in those days the responsibilities of a County Court judge were not onerous; the highest award he could make was £50. Another possibility is that he cut a poor figure in court; on the few occasions when I heard him address an audience his own overwhelming embarrassment was so communicable that the wit and aptness of what he was saying must have gone almost wholly for nothing, and the sight of a jury might well have unmanned him in much the same way. Whatever the cause, Ruth and I were given to understand from the first that poverty was the badge of our family and we must not expect to have what we saw others having; we even heard odd allusions to this much being owed to one tradesman and that much to another, and the children of the house were less dismayed than the servants when two bailiffs appeared at the front door and proceeded to carry out the copper warming-pan from the hall.

On the morning after the signing of the Armistice in November 1918 I heard strange sounds coming from my mother's bedroom. No one was willing at the time to tell me what they meant, but later in the day I found myself a guest in my grandfather's house about a quarter of a mile away, and those in charge of me gave me the answer. I now had a little sister — Penelope, as she was to be christened a few days afterwards. 'So you're no longer the baby of the family,' they added, 'and you've got to stop wetting your bed.' Alas, what they saw as a plain duty to be put off no further was the one thing in the world I most earnestly wanted to do; that recurrent misdemeanour was the sorrow and the shame of my life, and I would have given all the toys I had never had to rid myself of it; but even as they spoke I knew that I couldn't obey them. It was no fun being a bed-wetter in those days, for however cogently you argued your case the minds of your judges were already made up: you had just been too lazy to get out of bed. It never seemed to occur to anyone that if the need had been urgent enough to wake a child up it was unlikely to let him go easily back to sleep again — very occasionally perhaps it might have done so, but not night after night after night, with never the faintest memory of it in the morning. At some point in this period I was moved to a bedroom with a window open to the view of anyone coming up the hill, and whenever I had disgraced myself my bedclothes would be hung from the window-sill to dry, proclaiming to the neighbourhood that the dirty little boy at Limpsfield had done it again. It was all hopelessly confusing: I must be in the wrong, because all my elders said I was, yet at the same time I must be in the right, because I and only I knew the truth; so that my mind was perpetually torn by the irresoluble conflict between guilt and resentment.

By my second year at Culcheth another form of resentment was making itself increasingly felt: I was being denied the rights of my virility. The garment I had to wear in summer was not a shirt but a blouse; if I protested against being lugged into a compartment labelled For Ladies Only I was told that that was all right, I didn't count. And inevitably much of this resentment was directed against Culcheth itself: child I might be, but like Job I was at least a manchild, and a manchild should not be numbered overlong with the womenchildren. I took strong exception to the nature walks: hazel-catkins had no place in the upbringing of a man proper. I took even stronger exception to the games: I hated the ladylike basketball or netball or whatever it called itself; I hated the prissy French and English; and above all I hated the feminine travesty of cricket known as stoolball, of which my last memory is being bowled by a girl for nought.

In the end even my parents saw that the time had come for me to be sent to a real boys' school.

Wadham House School, Hale, was some two miles away: no small double trudge for a child of eight, but the children of those days took that sort of thing in their stride, even if the stride was as short as mine. On my way I used to pass Bowdon College, which was less than half a mile from my home, but then Bowdon College wasn't a preparatory school. Its headmaster, the fierce old Pike Smith, would glower at me from his front gate as I passed; he knew my father and he knew who I was, and I used to wince at that glowering. 'It's not my fault, sir,' I wanted to tell him, 'it's really not my fault.'

At first I was, of course, delighted by the change. I had at last been granted my true status in life, and I had been promoted from Michael to Longson — which is to say that I was addressed as one grown man of the period would be regularly addressed by another. But once the novel had become familiar I gradually became aware that I wasn't settling down at Wadham House, there was always something vaguely oppressive about its atmosphere; very probably I just didn't like most of the boys much, I can't say why. Not that I remember any overt bullying there, beyond the odd kick on the bottom or twisting of the arm; there was a potential masculine equivalent of my old deskmate at Culcheth, a red-faced heavy-weight with all the makings of a more than adequate pincher or worse, but I never heard of his doing anything as nasty as he clearly was; and the only maltreatment I was personally subjected to was at the hands of a boy a year my junior, who affronted my venerable eight and a half years by publicly and expeditiously outwrestling me when himself a mere infant of seven. I can still feel the dis-comfort of the schoolyard gravel beneath my outraged head.

Of the masters I remember only two, a middle-aged sandy-bearded man called Mr. Wood, and a large, briskly assertive man called Major Pears; had I stayed longer I might be able to tell of teachers far more effective than they, but if there was anyone of the calibre of Miss Craig or Mrs. Soutar on the staff I never came across him. On the evidence of my best friend the general standard of education at Wadham House was low; throughout his time at the school he had been the recognised number two of his year, yet when he was about twelve the vicar calling on his family was so badly shocked by the son of the house's ignorance that he reported his views to the parents, and my friend was transferred without delay to a school in the south known to specialise in desperate cases. On the other hand a famous High Court judge sent both his sons to Wadham House, and one of them became a High Court judge in his turn.

It was at Wadham House that my long devotion to Latin first made itself apparent, but that would have happened anyway. I have never quite understood how I came to recognise thus early that Latin and I were going to be friends; apart from the raw material there was no obvious affinity, no clear identity in kind, between the language of Ritchie's 'First Steps' and that of the *Aeneid* or the Lenten *Improperia*. Initially no doubt my enthusiasm came from the pleasure of exercising a newly-discovered faculty which my fellows couldn't rival, but it led by degrees to a deeper form of satisfaction. One day, on meeting another boy wearing my cap, my grandfather asked him if he knew a chap called Longson. 'Oh yes, sir!' answered the boy. 'He's a great Latin scholar.' My grandfather loved telling this story: according to his own account he enjoyed the irony of a description appropriate to a Bentley or a Lachmann, say, being solemnly applied by one small boy to another. I liked the story too, but for a more straightforward reason: I had been given my due.

It must also have been somewhere about the same time that I found I was something of a musician. There was never any suggestion of my becoming a virtuoso pianist; like the ability to draw a likeness, that basic technical fluency is something which you either have or have not — nor can it be dismissed as a purely physiological matter of coordination between brain and muscles, for too many of the composers have possessed it in a high degree — and it was always plain that I had it not. No, what I found out was that if anybody played or sang me a tune, provided that it was diatonic and reasonably simple, I could always reproduce it without fumbling on the piano; and by studying the chords in the hymn-book I soon taught myself to supplement the melody with a crude harmony of my own devising. Within a few years I was able to extend this modest accomplishment by learning to play harmonically as well as melodically by ear, and before I left school I had acquired a fair mastery of counterpoint. With this theoretical equipment, the limited technique which I developed over the years, and a copious store of good tunes such as civilised people usually like to listen to, I eventually became an acceptable social pianist; I also became an adequate organist for use in times of emergency. But I owe none of this to Wadham House.

What I do owe to Wadham House is the friendship of a lifetime.

As I struggled into my boots at the end of my first day I casually called out 'Does anybody else go home along South Downs Road?' and one voice answered 'Yes, I do.' That was the beginning of an association which if Alan had only managed to live twelve little months longer would have lasted for sixty years.

Alan Cameron Gilg was the only son, and far and away the youngest child, of a Swiss cotton merchant and a Scotswoman of good lineage. In 1919 Manchester cotton had still a few years of prosperity to run, and Hurstdene, South Downs Road, was a large though unbeautiful house with an imposing drive and sumptuous gardens; it was only half the distance from our school that Limpsfield was, so that there were two decisive reasons for our doing our habitual playing on his premises rather than mine. Our amusements in that first winter were harmless enough; the chief one so far as I can remember was the coloured reproduction, under Miss Lomax's indulgent eye, of the map of Europe in Professor

9

Meiklejohn's Atlas; we were fascinated by exotic names like Bosnia and Herzegovina which we had never heard of before and were unlikely to hear of again, for a whole Great War had been fought since the Professor published his monumental record. In one of the early weeks of our friendship I was maladroit enough to address a member of the household in a *sotto voce* which was less *sotto* than I supposed (it must have been that, for I should never have allowed myself on outside territory the licence that I enjoyed as a matter of course in my own less conventional home), and my muttered 'Mind your own business' was faithfully reported to the management. On our way back from school next day I became gradually aware that my friend was being more silent than usual, as one labouring with a message that he found it hard to deliver. In the end out it came, in halting, painfully rehearsed phrases — 'Betty told Mummy . . . and Mummy told Daddy . . . ' — and the upshot was that I was forbidden the house. The crisis did not as it turned out survive my distressful return home for long; that was the sort of affair that my mother was very good at dealing with, and after a short and amicable intermaternal exchange on the telephone I was re-admitted to favour.

Alan's mother died that same winter (a beautiful woman; I wish I could have known her on equal terms), and in 1926 his father died too, leaving the ruins of a business behind him. There was, as it happened, enough capital remaining to see the boy through his schooldays, though probably not enough for the university career which was his intellectual birthright; but the family took needless fright, removed him from Haileybury before he had even sat his School Certificate, and then added madness to madness by apprenticing him to a cotton-firm in Liverpool. Within four or five years the Liverpool firm collapsed too, and there he was in his early twenties, half-educated, with no job in prospect. He had the qualities for a responsible executive post; the power to make firm decisions, an acute intelligence capable of handling a multiplicity of detail on a large scale, integrity, conscientiousness and loyalty in abundance, all these were his to give; but he had nothing on paper to show for them. Apart from one colourful episode to be recorded later, his next seven years were years of unrelieved and demoralising frustration; then quite suddenly his luck changed, and he was invited to run the estate of an Oxfordshire landowner called Major Ford. From then on my friend became at last the happy man he was always meant to be. He had not only work to do, but honourable work of a kind that he liked doing and knew he could do well; his affable good-nature, his transparent genuineness and his quiet but lively humour quickly brought him a troop of exceptional friends, and above all he chose himself a nonpareil of a wife in Barbara Oakey, later to bear him three fine sons. Major Ford died during the war, but Alan found new congenial employment with the equally appreciative Frasers of Westhide, near Hereford; at Westhide indeed he was given an even wider scope for the exercise of his talents than he had had before, and his name soon commanded general respect among all who knew anything about farming in Herefordshire. I was his best man and the godfather of his eldest son Ian, and till his death in 1978 never a year went by without my spending at least one contented visit at Westhide. You have by no means heard the last of Alan Gilg.

By early 1920 my father had conceived doubts as to whether Wadham House was the place for his purposes: if I was to get to a public school I had to win a scholarship to take me there, and it was beginning to appear unlikely that I should be able to do that from any local establishment. Meanwhile he was hearing good reports of Mr. Dealtry's school in Hoylake from his old *Manchester Guardian* friend the playwright, novelist and critic Allan Monkhouse, who had married my mother's first cousin Dorothy: their elder son Paddy had won a high scholarship from The Leas to Rugby, and the younger Johnny was promising equally well. On some day in the spring, accordingly, my parents set off to see Mr. Dealtry.

The interview ran smoothly for a while, and then something went wrong: I fancy one of my parents was impelled to mention that I was still not wholly to be trusted in a bed. Anyhow the black cap was already in sight when my mother cried out in desperation, 'Oh, Harold, what *are* we to do? You see, Mr. Dealtry, he has an elder sister, and she stops him from concentrating on his homework.' Not for nothing was P.S. Dealtry known as one of the best headmasters in the north. 'Do you mean to say he *wants* to concentrate?' he said. From that moment I was in; with that moment there came into being the partnership of Dealtry and Longson, first as headmaster and pupil, then as gratified headmaster and successful pupil, and eventually as friend and friend.

But I mustn't forget my first cricket season, the season that was to show what manner of fruit that long training in the garden, with my father lobbing a tennis ball at me from five yards' distance, had eventually borne. In terms of runs scored the fruit was not particularly impressive; I had a habit of getting run out before my innings was properly under way, for my legs were never much and they had a fat little weight to carry at that time. On the last games day of the term the word went round that X had scored a run, and the news stiffened my resolve: 'Right then,' I said to myself, 'I also will score a run today.' But I didn't; I got run out again instead, and my aggregate for the year 1920 remained at 2.

Some forty years later I noticed the name of my old school on the front page of a Sunday newspaper: there had been a terrible fire in a timber-built hotel in Paris, and the victims included a party of schoolboys from Wadham House School, Hale. From what I have since gathered there was no blame attached to the school, but after a catastrophe like that nobody had the heart to carry on. Our playing fields are now built over, and the only memorial to the establishment is a road which runs where no road used to run, and which bears the name of Wadham Way.

HOYLAKE

Nicholas Monsarrat's account in his autobiography of The Leas, Hoylake, is that of a bleak and gaunt institution where he always had a cold and was nearly always miserable. My own distant retrospect is widely different from his, though there was only a year between us. I had some minor difficulties to face in my first three terms and a major one in my fourth, but once they were over I was well contented to be where I was. I wept as well as anybody on my last morning when the hymn came to 'Let Thy father hand be shielding Those who here shall meet no more,' and I gratefully accepted my two chances to return there as a temporary master between my finally leaving school and my leaving Oxford.

· I would agree with Monsarrat that the situation of the school exposed it to any wind that cared to blow in its direction, and it could be argued that the school song's 'Far over the golden sands of Dee Stand the purple hills outlined' is a less than honest description of the dingy estuary we knew and the grim little black hills we could see beyond it. But there wasn't much bleakness about the school itself; the building was mostly a cheerful blend of red brick and pale grey pebble-dash, and it had an expansive playing-field with a fair sprinkling of trees, partially bordered by a pleasant vegetable garden along one side and a nine-hole golf-course along the other.

Monsarrat's recollections are inevitably coloured by a traumatic experience of his own. As his book tells, one night in the dormitory he gave an utterly innocent answer to a question about one of the servants; his answer was overheard, misinterpreted and reported by the master on duty; the offence was publicly denounced next morning by one of the headmasters, who both held strong views on the dignity of servants; and for some reason or other — it cannot have been genuine indignation, for the ordinary Leasian wasn't in the least interested in the dignity of servants, indeed his own word for them was skivvies — the school understood this harangue as giving them a licence to inflict on the offender the barbaric

13

punishment known as running the gauntlet — that is running naked the full circuit of the gymnasium while they stood round and flicked their wet towels at his passing figure. But if Monsarrat was cruelly unfortunate in being the victim, it was also bad luck for The Leas that the victim should have been its one best-selling author. The episode was in no way typical of the school: in all my four years its like had never happened before and was never to happen again, and even at the time there must have been many of us who may well have carried wet towels for fear of the people, but had no intention whatsoever of using them. My own memory is of watching the scene with some dismay from afar, and I shouldn't have dared to do that if there hadn't been a reasonable quorum round me. That one discreditable performance apart, I saw no more of physical bullying at The Leas than I had at Wadham House. Mental bullying, yes: but that will have to wait.

It must be admitted that there was a slightly oppressive air of Victorian puritanism about the school that P.S. Dealtry and C.J.H. Barr founded between them about the turn of the century. Dealtry had more than a touch of genius, he was a convinced idealist and a stimulating, even inspiring, teacher, alive, humane and wise. Barr was also a man of high principles — though the principles were different in quality from Dealtry's, narrower and more rigid — and the mere fact of his holding the friendship and unquestioned regard of Dealtry for so many years suggests that somewhere within him was hidden a person very unlike the one he chose to let us see; he was certainly devoted to his calling, and certainly a most able and industrious administrator. The resultant ethos, which may of course have been shaping us more than we knew, wasn't very perceptibly reflected in most of our conscious thinking or our day-to-day behaviour; it was reflected rather in the atmosphere by which we felt ourselves surrounded, in the homilies addressed to us, the astringent attitudes shown towards us by authority, the general sense that we mustn't expect life to be a very comfortable thing.

The most remarkable example of this basic austerity was the programme arranged for our Saturday evenings. We were assured — quite sincerely as I believe, though some of the more cynical may have had their doubts — that The Leas didn't believe in prizes; in compensation we should be given an entertainment every Saturday night, summer terms excepted, either with the school cinematograph or with the school magic lantern. In practice we had roughtly one Monty Banks or Tin Lizzy comedy for every three lantern lectures. Instead of getting a treat we were fobbed off with yet another lesson, usually in my unfavourite subject of geography; by the time I was ten I had been shown enough about rubber plantations and Indian villages to sate me for a lifetime. The cold baths and the food were at least expectable.

It is not really fair to cite the cold baths as an example of austerity. They presumably did us some good, and they weren't particularly rigorous: you jumped in, you immersed yourself momentarily, and you clambered out again; that was all. We had moreover our own way of evading them. If you were asked 'Have you had a cold bath?' you answered 'Yes', because you had at some time or other had one; if you were asked 'Have you had a cold bath today?' you answered 'Yes, today', because phonematically that was the same as 'Yesterday'; and if you hadn't had one the day before you just said 'Yes', for you knew quite well that in any case you were really telling a lie. It says much about the weight of public opinion with the young that this convention was accepted without demur even by such a one as myself, who was so scrupulously veracious in all other matters that if I was sent to fetch something from another room and failed to find it I wouldn't report on my return 'I can't find it,' for just possibly I might have found it if I had looked better: I would say 'I don't see it.'

The asker of the question, suitably enough, would be either Jackie Barr or Lum-lum. Jackie was the prime representative of the Spartan tradition at The Leas; in the worst of weathers he was never seen wearing any kind of overcoat, and on these mornings he would march from dormitory to dormitory clad only in pyjamas, with the jacket open at the neck (which was uncommon in those days), and not tucked inside the trousers as ours were. Lum-lum was from ages back the school matron, though she would never have claimed the social standing that the term implies. She was a quaint, wizened little figure, with a twisted face and a perpetually running eye; she evidently believed that boys should be brought up the hard way, and she rarely spoke to them without some degree of asperity. She had nevertheless a gentle side which young Monsarrat was lucky and shrewd enough to discover; and there must have been a firm bond of mutual loyalty and affection between her and Dealtry, for when I visited the old man in his retirement years afterwards there she was as his housekeeper, a friendly Lum-lum now.

The food was a very different matter, for here ethical theory may well have been reinforced by economic. We could have either butter or jam on our bread, but very, very seldom both together, and though I for one saw this at the time as just one illustration of the law that we weren't to expect too much of life, in retrospect it is clear that the decisive consideration could have been fiscal. The

15

so-called scrambled eggs, which we knew as egg slush and which one master ate with a spoon, could be excused on the ground that the real thing would have been impossible to prepare on so large a scale; but nothing could have excused the Monday morning ham. We dreaded Mondays because of that ham: the fat was something between yellowish and greyish, the lean limp and slimy with grease; the more adroit carried tins into which they scooped their helpings for later disposal, and at the age of twelve I cried when a master ordered me to eat mine up.

The daily routine was much the same as it would have been at a thousand other schools, except that twice a week the morning break was diverted from its rightful purpose to be used for company drill — a concession, I imagine, to the wishes of Mr. (ex-Major) Sutton. The main ritual was that of morning prayers, which were held in the dining hall. The two headmasters presided at a long table in front of us; behind them to one side sat the music mistress or Mr. Sutton at the harmonium and to the other the assistant masters in their long easy chairs, while at right angles, on small hard chairs, sat the troop of maidservants which Lum-lum led in from the pantry door. The hymns I remember were usually Victorian hymns of the third water, 'O Paradise, O Paradise!', 'Art thou weary, art thou languid?', 'Hark, hark, my soul, angelic songs are swelling'; why they were chosen I have never understood, for their sentiments made little appeal to the congregation and were quite alien to the ascetic Christianity of our governors. The tunes too: I can't say that they created that regrettable taint in my musical taste from which I have been striving to cleanse it ever since, but they must surely have helped to foster it. We had of course our favourite hymns. 'The Son of God goes forth to war' we welcomed because 'A noble army, men and boys, The matron and the maid' mirrored so precisely the company present in that hall, but most of the favourites were liked because of their tunes: 'Onward, Christian soldiers' to St. Gertrude and 'All hail the power of Jesus' name' to Miles' Lane are the two that come most readily to mind. Yet even over Miles' Lane the censor had to step in: all the verses but one were sung in the same way as those of any other common metre hymn, with no repetitions, no broadening of the time-values in the fourth line, no exhilarating climax; only in the last verse were we allowed to satisfy our frustrations with an exultant 'Crown Him, crown Him, crown Him, crown Him Lord of all!'

On Sundays our morning devotions were paid at the local parish church, whither we were marched in Eton suits and where we had our own private chapel, so that school prayers were held in the evening, at that hour of the week when the spirit of man is apt to be at its lowest. The harmonium was now played by Mrs. Dealtry, a small and frail-looking woman who was plainly of a distinguished cast, but plainly also a sad and vulnerable person. Rumour had it that she was under sentence of death, and her son Tim told me some time afterwards that rumour had not erred: she had been living in constant fear for ten years before she learnt that the diagnosis was a bad one. With her the harmonium gave a quieter and thinner sound than it did with either of our week-day accompanists, perhaps because her legs were too weak to force enough air into the instrument, perhaps because she didn't dare to ask more of her resources, and its plaintive tones echoed and added to the prevailing mood of depression. The most dangerous hymn was one sung to a tune by Ebenezer Prout, which with its long-drawn-out notes at the end of the second line and the beginning of the last embodied in itself the very essence of nostalgia:

> Holy Father, in Thy mercy
>   Hear our anxious prayer;
> Keep our loved ones, now far absent,
>   'Neath Thy care.
>
> When in sorrow, when in danger,
>   When in loneliness,
> In Thy love look down and comfort
>   Their distress.

Many an eye was secretly moistened as we sang those words; but it wasn't for our deprived loved ones that we were grieving, it was for our deprived little selves.

Of the masters and mistresses who took me in my first two years three stand out: Mr. Sutton, Miss Stocqueler and Mr. Vaughan.

K.H.M. Sutton was the most complex and interesting figure of the three. He had a fine head already thinning on the top, and a handsome face with blue eyes and brown military moustache; the size and power of his well-carried body won our universal admiration; he thrilled us at school concerts with a ringing and sympathetic baritone the like of which I have never heard from any other amateur, and he wrote in an exquisite and individual hand which many of us strove hard and in vain to copy. He undoubtedly knew his job: we remembered what he told us, and he had a fair knowledge of the classical languages he taught, though he was not considered under either of the Dealtry régimes, as he was under a

17

later one, enough of a scholar to be given any of the top work. He commanded our little corps in its Wednesday and Saturday morning parades, and unofficially at least he ran the school music. But his success was partly based on fear, for he was possessed by a brooding ill-humour which could at any moment rise to a truly formidable anger; he would march round the room to look over our shoulders at what we were writing, and his 'You are idle, boy, idle!' would be emphasised by a clap of his huge fist about our ears. I doubt if the charge was often true, I doubt if many boys would have dared to be positively *idle* under Sut: we let our concentrations slip a little sometimes, that was all. Only now and then was the atmosphere lightened, when he may have been in a better mood or a chance remark from a boy may have amused him; on these occasions a little twinkle would come into the blue eyes, and the gleam of a wintry geniality would show briefly through.

A few years after I left, when Dealtry had been succeeded by his son Tim, a new music mistress was so much worried by his persistent grumblings that she asked him outright, 'Will you tell me what you find wrong with my work, Mr. Sutton?' He turned away without a word, strode to his car, drove to the masters' house two-thirds of a mile off, and returned an hour later with a closely typed letter which he handed to her, again without a word. She was still in tears over that letter when she was discovered by the headmaster's wife, who of course had to be told the story. 'Don't worry, my dear,' she said. 'We all have to put up with him.'

I fancy that Sutton was obsessed with the idea of what might have been, or rather what he wished had been, and even that his habitual aggressiveness masked the self-mistrust of a man whose achievements had never come up to his hopes. He may or may not have tried and failed to become a professional singer, but in any case it is likely that his highest and deepest ambitions were musical. Before the one Easter Day that came in term-time while I was at The Leas we were convened for a special congregational practice to learn a new hymn at a prescribed pitch; Sutton was the accompanist, and his performance was uncharacteristic. He and I happened to be washing our hands together afterwards in the same changing-room, and rather to my surprise he was grateful to see who his neighbour was. 'Do you know why I played that hymn so badly?' he said. 'Yes, sir. You were asked to play it in a different key from the one in the book.' 'That's it, I had to transpose. You'll never go very far in music if you can't transpose.' You'll never go very far ... that revealed much, at least it does now. A great deal too can be explained by his premature deafness; his failures could have weighed less heavily on him, he could have been a very different

18

person, had his mind not been driven in on itself by that enforced semi-isolation. He was an unhappy man.

I find it harder to forget all feuds when I come to Miss Stocqueler. Grey-haired, bespectacled, alert and intelligent, she was a kind of Miss Silver without the wisdom or the benevolence. She too had probably been saddened, perhaps even embittered, by experience; but while she was like Sutton in drawing some partial compensation from the exercise of her professional skills and the ascendancy she held over her classes, unlike him she had her feelings well under control: if ever she gave play to them it was of her own choice. Whatever her hidden troubles may have been, there was no need for her to take them out quite so systematically on small boys who couldn't answer her back: she was under no compulsion, for instance, to reprimand a boy who had suffered from bad circulation since his birth, and took a natural interest in the consequent colour of his hands, with 'Get on with your work, Longson, and stop admiring your lumps of raw beef.' Barr and Lum-lum, as we vaguely understood, were strict with us on some sort of principle: Stocqueler was unkind because she wanted to be.

After at least two terms of Sutton and Stocqueler it was necessary for the balance of the scheme that there should be some more liberal influence at work in the middle of the school, and appropriate therefore that the master in charge of the Fourth Form should have been C.G. Vaughan, or Foghorn as he was generally called — a clever nickname, for as well as being an affectionate pun on his name it paid tribute to that stentorian sneeze of his which from time to time reverberated along our corridors. There was no nonsense about him and he would have stood for none; he was bluff, forthright and friendly, and he could teach. He was in no sense an intellectual — though he had a brother at Oxford or Cambridge, indeed many years later Tim Dealtry cunningly exploited the connection to win him an obituary in *The Times* — but in most of the ways that mattered he was a very good schoolmaster.

Perhaps I should have added a fourth name, for I seem to remember that I first came across Mr. Hadley in the Third Form; he may even have been its form-master in addition to his higher commitments. Somebody must have given me a grounding in Latin verse before I reached the First, and I don't think it would have been Sutton; conceivably, but not very probably, I taught myself by noticing the details of what I was reading, much as I had more consciously done in learning the elements of harmony. At all events Hadley's true place in my story is not here.

Most of my personal history in those first two years was uneventful and can be soon told.

Because of a contagious skin complaint my arrival was delayed by three weeks, so that I missed the initial test and was in consequence placed not in the Fifth of our seven forms, but in the inferior Sixth, under Miss Beckerleg. (They had queer names, our three mistresses. Miss Stocqueler, Miss Beckerleg and Miss Quirk: they could have made a good key-line for a song, like the Argentine and the Portuguese and the Greek of the Duncan Sisters' record.) I was promoted to the Fifth in January and spent two terms in it; thereafter my promotion was terminal, which means that by the end of my second year I was ready for admission to the top form. My performance throughout was beaten by that of a boy called Smith; I was probably the better classic, but he had the double advantage of being a competent mathematician and being prepared to work at the subjects that didn't interest him.

In my first term I won some prestige to begin with from the fact that I was cousin to the great Monkhouse, the captain of most things and already within a few months of assuming his five-term reign as Head of the School; but I soon learnt that basking in reflected glory was among the more transient human pleasures, the business of justifying your existence rested in the end with yourself. I enjoyed also the privilege allowed to all new boys of breakfasting at Dealtry's own table, and my account of how he would address me with 'Fatty, I'm sure you'll bust' has shaken many people familiar only with the slender or even gaunt figure of the later me. But the supreme moment came when I was introduced to 'Lo, He comes' at our last congregational practice, for it was a glorious tune and it stood for Advent, and all that Advent could possibly mean was the approach of the Christmas holidays.

It was in my fourth term that I ran into trouble. I was now in the Long Dorm — there were thirteen boys in it — and on no pretext whatsoever I found myself becoming the butt for the nightly verbal persecution of a few ill-wishers. Their leader was an overgrown oaf of a boy from Bowdon, who doubtless considered me vulnerable game because he knew from his parents that my own were badly off — though they had perhaps been less ready to mention that they were themselves classed as *nouveaux riches*. To tell my tale properly I should be able to describe my sufferings in detail, to say 'Thus and thus did they unto me', but as it is I only remember that the oppression was ruthless and continuous, and that I spent a thoroughly unhappy term because of it. Eventually it was my mother who came to the rescue.

In many ways she was far from the kind of mother a schoolboy would have chosen to have, especially when she appeared at the school itself. If there was a wrong thing she could do she was always agog to do it: at Eton, for instance, she had to be dissuaded from violating the sanctity of Sixth Form Passage by 'just popping in' to an august room 'to see what it was like'. She was dangerously intolerant of the childproud parent, and if some rival mother at a school function insisted on telling her what all the masters said about dear Jimmy she responded with a frigid disparagement of her own Michael; but of course the withering rebuke was never seen as such, only as an unexpectedly concessive admission of defeat. Her attitude towards myself was for the most part exceptionally undemonstrative, and I would rather have her like that than like two Bowdon parents we knew of, who on the last day of their sons' holidays would give them all their favourite foods and ensure that they won all the family games, then jointly see them off at the station on the morrow, the father weeping as openly as the mother — even if I did sometimes feel that there must be some sort of a mean between such abject emotionalism as that and her brusque 'Goodbye and good riddance.' But whenever I really needed her motherliness I had it, and never was it more acceptably shown than in her nightly visits to my bedroom during my first few holidays from The Leas. On the night when she heard of what had been happening in the Long Dorm she was not only deeply sympathetic and indignant, she was also decisive: something would have to be done.

Within one or two weeks she received Dealtry's answer to her letter. The dormitories were being reorganised — no negligible feat of administration, and no small break in Barr's holidays — and if I felt at all 'low' when I got back I was to go and see Dealtry himself.

As it turned out the new term didn't start quite as smoothly as I had hoped, and I went and saw him on the first morning.

'Well?'

'Please, sir, I'm feeling rather low.'

'Well, what is it?' Dealtry's tone was abrasive. 'Has someone been nasty to you, or what?'

'Yes, sir ... but I can't tell you who it was, sir.'

'Oh, don't be silly, boy. I won't *do* anything to him. But surely you see that I must know what's wrong. Who was it?'

So I gave him the name of a chubby, red-faced boy with spectacles, for those reasons known as Pickwick; and the boy was duly summoned.

'Ah, Pickwick! Pickwick, I think you may be the man we want. There's poor Poppy here: he's a nice old thing really, but he does

21

rather need someone to help him a bit at the moment. Will you be that someone?'

Pickwick accepted the commission proudly, and he and I walked out of the study good friends already. In fact I had no further trouble in my relations with other people throughout the rest of my time at The Leas.

Dealtry and Barr had done their work well, and for a good while the Long Dorm was a happy dorm. It was especially so on Mutt story nights. Mutt Clark was a small lively boy, of no great academic pretensions but gifted with a rare power of improvising on request the most imagination-gripping of fantasies. Someone would say 'What about a Mutt story?', the rest of us would chorus 'Yes, yes, Mutt: please!', and the story would immediately follow. He never failed to comply with our entreaties, and his invention never let him or us down. But even from the reformed Long Dorm the evil spirit had not been wholly exorcised; in the summer there arose a new set of persecutors, and they required a new victim. He was a quiet and pleasant enough boy so far as I could see, and he probably knew no more of what he had done to offend than I had known in my own case. This time the persecution did at least once take a physical form: not in itself a very brutal form, for there is nothing particularly painful about being thrust down on your bed and knelt upon, but applied in that context and that spirit it was cruel indeed. On these occasions too I was a watcher from afar, and I don't think it consciously occurred to any of us that we might protest. I had indeed done something of the kind myself not many months before, when the big senior boy in charge of our changing-room had been sadistically baiting one of my contemporaries, and my dauntless 'You are a bully, So-and-so!' had shamed him into decency. But perhaps it takes less courage to stand up to a single senior boy in the knowledge that all the spectators are behind you than to confront a group of the dormitory-mates you have to live with, and perhaps that was why I chose not to think of intervening.

That second summer term was also my third cricket season, and I was beginning to wonder what kind of cricketer I was shaping to be; there was nothing remarkable in my record hitherto, but the case was still *sub judice*. Like those of many other small boys my ambitions were high: by now I was seeing the occasional match at Old Trafford, and I aspired to something more impressive than my father's mere club level. I knew I wasn't much good at most physical activities — I was no gymnast, I couldn't run or jump, if I ever tried to dribble a soccer ball I was invariably dispossessed by the first comer — but I hadn't yet realised that you couldn't expect to excel in any one game if you didn't show an at least respectable aptitude for games in general. I knew too that I was deficient in one of the skills specifically demanded by cricket, for to my deep and lasting humiliation I could only throw the ball in the way that girls threw it; but even that disability might be overcome if only I could make myself a good enough wicket-keeper to be given the job more often than not. This line of reasoning was not so unrealistic as it may seem, for wicket-keeping in those days was mostly a more sedate business than it is now; a great deal of it consisted in standing up to the wicket and taking the off-side ball clean, and even when keeping to McDonald I can't remember that Duckworth ever had to dive much. I was still prepared at that time to find out in the end that my dreams had only been dreams, but I continued to polish my forward stroke and to work at my up-to-the-wicket taking in the hope that some day they might be realised.

Meanwhile there were changes going on at home.

My mother's search for a suitable cook-general had ended with the establishment in the kitchen of Lily Wroe. Lily was a Salvationist, but scarcely a representative one, indeed she may have caused some concern among her militant colleagues; for though she used to stand in the middle of Altrincham singing 'I stroodle and pray' in a gurgly soprano, she didn't always stroodle and pray quite hard enough. She had a wooden tablet on her kitchen wall bearing in pokercraft the maxim 'Don't worry. It may never happen'; but in her case it *had* happened, and some years later, when she was no longer in our employ, it happened again — though that time the sire was from a different stable. Where she housed her child I cannot say, but she clearly kept a maternal eye on it, for she was proud enough of it to send its photograph in to a babies' beauty competition, with the mother's name candidly attached. I knew nothing of all this, though Ruth may well have done, and to our parents it was only relevant in so far as my father made sure that the man paid her alimony. To the family at large she was deeply loyal and devoted, and her robust Lancashire humour and robust Lancashire horse-sense made her an invaluable member of the household. She was also my mother's most trusted adviser. When my mother held an afternoon party for some ten of Ruth's Culcheth friends and could devise no means of entertaining them once the tea had been eaten, it was to the kitchen that she fled with her despairing plea: 'Lily, what *am* I to do with them?' 'Turn 'em out into t'yard,' was the practical answer. It was a pity that she came across the one entry I have ever made in a diary: 'Lily tried to do rock-cakes today. They were a terrible mess.'

A somewhat later addition to the staff was Penelope's new nurse, a buxom farmer's daughter called Madge Wilson. Madge was a lovely person. She had all the natural dignity and the ancient breeding of the Cumbrian yeomanry; she was endlessly good-natured and good-tempered, yet I should have felt it somehow wrong to try on with her the easy pleasantries that did well enough for my bouts with Lily. She must also, of course, have had some life of her own outside the family at Limpsfield. She was waiting at our table on the occasion of Penelope's first being allowed to stay up for Christmas dinner, and she was plainly confused when under the new stimulus of wine Penelope pointedly and repeatedly asked her, 'Madge, what about Bert Yarwood?' But alas, we never learnt what about Bert Yarwood, nor what about any successor or successors he may have had, and when Penelope looked her up in her Ambleside cottage many years afterwards she found only a grey, attenuated old woman, drained of all the life and the warm humanity of the Madge Wilson she had known.

In the garden Edie and Johnny had been replaced — I hope for no illiberal reason, but I wouldn't swear to it — by our neighbours Clifford and Peter Denham. Cliff was a solid, down-to-earth, intelligent boy with all the makings of a successful business man, while Pete was a friendly little wisp of a thing with blue ingenuous eyes, whose major occupation was that of admiring his big brother. Cliff loved to tell us impressive stories of how lavishly they had just been entertained by their father in Manchester, and he could rely on me to give the right response. 'Oh, you *are* lucky!' I would sigh. '*We* never get anything like that!' 'You big silly,' Ruth would admonish me afterwards; 'they were only swanking. They weren't anywhere near the Palace last night.' I got the great Cliff down once, to my own surprise and Peter's vocal dismay, by applying a useful neck-hold of my own invention; that initial victory once achieved I was always quick to release my opponent before he had a chance of reversing the position, so poor Pete had to make do with a fallen idol for a day or two.

But my own chief playmate was still Alan Gilg. We were both great pretenders, and between us we hit upon the most satisfactory exercise in wish-fulfilment that I have ever known or heard of. His Hurstdene was one county cricket club and my Limpsfield another; each of us had ten successive innings with two differently named batsmen in at the two ends and the name of the newcomer announced at the fall of a wicket; we changed ends every six balls and the name of the bowler was always similarly announced; if any uppish stroke was made which was out of the bowler's reach the issue was settled by tossing up. He and I were, of course, the captains of our respective teams, and the Hurstdene captain usually scored more runs than the Limpsfield one; for whereas M.H. Longson always put himself in first and hoped for the best the shrewder A.C. Gilg preferred to bat at number four, when the corporate eye of his side was comparatively well in. Every time I rode round to Alan's house on my bicycle — a birthday present from my parents which even I had recognised at first sight as a repaint — I was the popular young captain driving to the opponents' county ground. It was all perfect.

When I got off my bicycle I would go up four broad steps to the imposing front door, and on my pressing the little button beside it a faint sound was audible from somewhere within. A maid would appear, gleaming in white cap and apron, greet me politely with 'Good morning, Master Michael. I will see if Master Alan is in', and make her noiseless way to the drawing-room door, from which she would announce: 'Master Alan, Master Michael is here.' But occasionally *he* came to see *me,* and when that happened I could feel myself blushing all over. The bell-wire would jangle stridently through the house, Lily's great feet would thump along the passage, the door would crash as it banged against the wall, and then came the bellow: 'MAHKOOL! 'ERE'S ULLUN!' Not till within a few months of his death did Alan let me know that of the two he had been the more deeply envious; he can't have had much fun in a household where family was family and staff was staff and never the twain should meet, and he would have loved to share the easy-going ways of Limpsfield.

To double the irony, within a very few years I was to be at Eton and he an office-boy in Liverpool; whereby hang many a noble quotation and many a discredited platitude, and they twain do indeed meet, with a quite disconcerting frequency.

I associate these encounters more with April than with August or September, for then we were both likely to be away with our families for much of the time. I resented those family holidays because they reduced my chances not only of playing cricket with Alan but of watching it at Old Trafford, and since I disliked walking and had no great interest either in bathing or in natural beauty I didn't feel I was getting much in the way of compensation. We always stayed in lodgings of some kind; my mother explained that only common people went to hotels, but the explanation accorded ill with the summary she gave in later years: '*We* didn't like the bad landladies, and the good landladies didn't like *us.*' One of the good landladies objected to our habit of leaving sandy shoes about her bedrooms, and expressed her disapproval by throwing the offending objects down before our eyes as we ate our lunch.

Our excursions were made by horse-drawn landaulette, and I enjoyed them because of the smell of the upholstery and the privilege of sitting beside the driver. What I have just said of my indifference to natural beauty can't have been wholly true, for I still vividly recall the sight of Lake Cwm Bwchan, a brilliant azure for once, with the great hills standing benignantly around it. In a group near us there was a striking blue-eyed man with a light red beard, and my mother exclaimed, 'Harold, the Messiah!' I half believed her; I didn't quite understand what she meant, but I was vaguely excited by the idea.

That holiday of 1921 almost brought my death. There was as yet no notice-board on the beach at Llanbedr warning bathers of the dangerous currents, and in my first year as a swimmer I had gone rather further out than I intended. 'Swim this way, Michael!' called Peggy Neatby. 'Swim towards *us!*' 'I'm trying to,' I puffed as I plied my newly learnt breast stroke, a little anxiously now. The man who eventually carried me to safety on his shoulders told my parents afterwards that he wouldn't have tried it if the water had been any deeper. Only two years before Ruth also had come near drowning at Llandudno; the danger there lay in the sudden steep shelving of the foreshore, which made it treacherous ground at high tide, and Ruth was going down for the third time when the boatman's pole hooked her bathing suit, while Miss Mercer and I looked on helplessly from the railings above.

In the Christmas holidays there was the pantomime, to which I was treated by an affluent great-aunt — no trivial matter, for you stood nowhere with your fellow near-Mancunians if you couldn't discuss the Transformation Scene — and the children's parties which I always dreaded in advance and usually ended by enjoying. But the principal events of the season were without question the Christmas and New Year family dinners.

The Christmas dinner was held at Limpsfield, with my grandfather and my aunts Dolly and Nora the guests, and the only memories that linger — apart from Penelope's curiosity about Bert Yarwood — are of the fascination I felt at the way my grandfather's shirt heaved and creaked in time with his wheezy breathing, and of one less than usually felicitous remark of my own. Aunt Dolly had a great friend called Miss Perry, who was a subject of great interest to Ruth and me because she wore a moustache, and I suddenly remembered that that was also the name of the music-mistress who had lately taken Miss Quirk's place at The Leas. 'We've got a new mistress this term, auntie,' I said; 'Her name's Miss Perry.' 'Oh?' said Aunt Dolly. 'Is she like our Perry?' 'No,' I replied cheerfully; 'she's clean-shaven.' That little sally was atoned for in tears shortly afterwards as Aunt Dolly sat brushing her hair in my mother's bedroom.

New Year's night was a very different affair, for the dinner was then at my grandfather's house and my father's brother Basil and his family were there. Uncle Basil never took much notice of either Ruth or me, but at those parties I worshipped him. His individual line in drollery would of itself have made them occasions to look forward to, but it was his musicianship that made them unforgettable. A messmate from his war days said of him, 'He was a brilliant long pianist' — an unusual phrase, but it hit off perfectly the way his hands would range over the compass of the whole keyboard in their rippling embellishments of whatever tune he happened to be playing. If the tune was that of a song then he would sing it too, and I can still see the look he threw over his shoulder as he encouraged the rest of us to join in. Alas, he died when I was fifteen, and on the following New Year's night I was called on to take his place. But I was nowhere near ready for it. My immature treble voice couldn't even be offered as a substitute for the virile tones with which he had led the singing, and my pianism, though it was reasonably accurate and musical, had none of the exhilarating flair they were all used to. When I ventured on a tune too closely associated with Uncle Basil somebody quickly interposed, 'No, Michael. Not that, please.' I was doubtless not alone in regretting the experiment, and I can't remember when it was next tried.

In the autumn of 1922 I became a member of the form in which I was to spend all the second half of my four years at The Leas. The form-master was I.A. Hadley, popularly known as Dodderer or Doddy; but it was an inept nickname, suggested only by his supposed antiquity, for there was nothing at all doddering about that spruce and active figure with the alert slate-grey eyes and the neatly trimmed moustache. He took us for all our Greek and English and shared the Latin reading with Dealtry himself, but he was allowed no part in our Latin compositions; this was a serious fault in the system which may well have impoverished the school's proud record of awards won, and if so nobody would have been more keenly aware of that than Hadley.

Dealtry always excepted, Hadley was the one master of unmistakable distinction at The Leas, and my life-long debt to him has been greater than I could ever have repaid in any form of currency. He was the gentleman-scholar at its old-fashioned best; he exemplified in himself the culture he stood for. I don't think he often used the word scholarship, but the idea of it, with the urbanity and fastidiousness it could combine, was implicit in every word he spoke, indeed it was reflected in his manner and his voice and the way he moved. There was a flavour of period about some of the things he said: it was he who told us that the mark of a gentleman's clothes was that you didn't notice them, and that it was in bad taste to write 'Rd.' instead of 'Road'; but the classic was speaking as well as the near-sexagenarian when he gave the name of his home town as Weston-super-Mary. When he introduced us to Housman's 'On an Army of Mercenaries', I suggested that the end might be more effective with a dash before the last two words. 'Some lady poets might have used one,' he answered. He could be mildly stern and even astringent if the occasion called for it; he too began an admonition with Miss Stocqueler's old words, 'Get on with your work, Longson,' but the second half of his was far more shrewdly aimed: 'and stop looking round for applause.' At other times it could be the very slightness of the rebuke that gave it its force. One day in my last year the junior boy behind me persistently goaded me by pressing with his foot against the rung of my chair; and when breaking-point came, I rose, turned, hurled my Xenophon at him from a range of fully two feet, scrambled over his desk to retrieve it with a furious 'Damn, it's missed!', came back to my seat and burst into tears. 'Tut tut, what language!' said Hadley: and the lesson went on again as I cried it out.

There were only two things wrong with Hadley's teaching so far as I know: he couldn't arouse enthusiasm as surely as he could stimulate interest, and like other good teachers I know of he had the bad habit of inculcating his own antipathies, which could mean his own limitations. Ovid and Pope, for instance, were 'mere versifiers'. Poetry was always poetry, and prose could be great prose, but verse was never more than just verse; Ovid and Pope therefore were reduced to the ranks of the irretrievably second-rate. Some six or seven years afterwards I found out for myself that there could indeed be great verse, and in due course I learnt that there were some poets who could range freely between good verse and great verse and poetry, and that the two most obvious examples were Ovid and Pope — though a case could also be made for the likes of John Betjeman and Shakespeare.

It was left to Dealtry to acquaint us with the emotional element in poetry. I won't claim that I was at all precociously sensitive in my response to the pathos in Virgil, but at least I was made aware that a sensitive response was possible, and I saw reason to hope that when I was old enough I should be able to give it. Dealtry himself was deeply and perceptibly moved by what we were reading, and he loved to recite Lord Bowen's version of the Marcellus passage in the Sixth Aeneid: 'Tell me not, O my son, of thy children's infinite pain.' I wish I could say that he also reawakened my old interest in history, but I had by then regarded the subject too long as a mere catalogue of events and reigns and dates: our text-books didn't help (Ed. J.S. Lay was a dull historian, and dull again as a geographer), and even Dealtry couldn't bring me to realise, as Miss Craig had done, that history was fundamentally about human beings, what they did and what happened to them. So I didn't work at it and I learnt little of it — a deficiency that was to cost me dear a few years later, and dearer still a few years after that.

Our Latin prose and verse, our mathematics and our geography were all in the hands of Jackie Barr.

I have already disclaimed any right to judge any teachers of maths, and perhaps on the ground of my personal hatred of geography I should disclaim any right to judge any teacher of that too; but I know that Barr taught it badly. I fancy that in our preps we were expected to read Ed.J.S. Lay, but I can't remember that the results were ever investigated. Every term all our lessons but two followed the same plan: he read aloud from a book, which may or may not have been by Mr. Lay, while we silently listened according to our several capabilities of so doing. The two exceptional lessons were devoted to the two fateful Tests, each consisting of fifty questions demanding one-word (or short phrase) answers. Towards the end of the period we exchanged papers, the official answer was given, and we marked one another. A question in one test was 'What load can a camel carry in the desert?', and I thought with relief, 'Ah, I can do that. I was listening then.' The answer was 500 pounds, and I was slightly piqued when my own offer of 5,000 tons was disallowed. Our terminal places in geography were decided solely by our showing in those two tests, so there was another subject in which I always came down.

In Latin prose Barr was probably adequate, for Caesar's plain and simple periods, though it took a great writer to devise them, were easy enough to imitate, so long as you knew and followed the rules. But Dealtry should never have let him loose on the Latin verse. His main qualification was that he carried with him a black, shiny book containing versions done by an admired brother at Cambridge, and the only line I remember from that thesaurus reversed the balance of the original sense, broke a cardinal law of syntax, and sounded horrid. Once he was mad enough to set us a quatrain from *The Gondoliers*:

In a contemplative fashion
And a tranquil frame of mind,
Free from every trace of passion,
Some solution let us find.

Anyone at all acquainted with the Ovidian style will know that it is largely based on solid clauses with verbs and subjects, if not objects, as well, and the problems posed by that serried row of abstract phrases, with their threefold expression of the same sense, could have been amusing material for a party game in the rooms of an Oxford don; to set them before a class of boys aged twelve or thereabouts was just irresponsible. Predictably no solution could any of us find, and for once no fair copy was produced; perhaps even the academic brother had declined the challenge. For our exams that term, my next-to-last incidentally, we were given a set of old scholarship papers kindly lent by Fettes College; in the Latin verse I got 60, Smith got 30, and none of the other eight got anything at all.

In the previous autumn Ruth too had gone away to boarding-school, at Liverpool College, Huyton. We saw her off at Broadheath station, looking forlorn and strangely pathetic as she leant out of the compartment window in her new uniform. Peggy Neatby and I went to a cinema afterwards to cheer ourselves up. One Saturday Ruth came to see me at The Leas on one of her week-end leaves, and I naturally looked forward to showing her off. Her visit went even better than I had hoped: the general reaction was highly appreciative, and what was most gratifying of all was the hit she made with C.J.H. Barr. I now saw a Jackie Barr utterly new to me: he was affable, he was charming, he was even gallant; he almost flirted with her. On the following Monday, when he was teaching us, somebody said something which made me give a short laugh. 'Stop giggling like a schoolgirl, Longson,' he said. 'You're not with your sister now.' It was my first taste of grown-up treachery, and I never forgave it him.

I have already confessed to having been mildly megalomaniac in my early youth, and the time has now come to reveal what form my megalomania took. I believed that I was a genius. There were doubtless other causes behind this aberration, congenital or adventitious or both, but I am inclined to associate it myself with an experience I had as a very young child. As I lay in bed one night I was struck with awe and wonder by the realisation that I was I, or to put it more precisely than I could have then, I was all that I directly knew, or could ever directly know, of human consciousness; surely, surely I must therefore be somebody very special indeed. Soon after I entered The Leas I decided that the somebody very special indeed was a genius of some kind, and by the time I had been a term or two in the First Form I knew what kind of genius I was: I was a great poet. The illusion was fostered by the fact that since no one shared my ambitions I had no competitors and therefore no criterion to judge myself by; I might have taken a humbler view of my own productions had I foreknown what quality of work that Maecenas of schoolmasters, W.G. Williamson, would elicit some decades later from the aspiring cygnets of Ashdown House; I should also have been less likely to regard myself as a second Beetle if I had been told, as I was to be told within one or two years, that the mature Kipling could throw off a perfect extempore limerick on the slightest provocation.[1] As it was, the fantasy was allowed to inflate itself at will. I never told my friends of my belief, I rarely thought much about it myself; yet of all my hopes this was the one that counted for most. I might or might not win a scholarship to Eton; once there I might or might not keep wicket at Lord's; but if I was a great poet I possessed a transcendent privilege that nothing and nobody could ever take away from me.

My other small talent, music, was recognised just as much as I liked, and no more. I sang in the odd group at concerts, and I once played the harmonium at Sunday prayers without causing more embarrassment than others had done before me. But my obvious want of technical facility saved me from having to play the piano in public when I wasn't quite up to it, a fate which befell my friend Pickwick.

Poor Pickwick. If anyone thinks the keyboard works of Haydn or Scarlatti dangerously simple, let him try 'The Old Gardener'. 'The Old Gardener' was what Bach might have called a two-part invention, in that each hand had only one note to play at a time; but the two parts were so many octaves away from each other that if

1. I owe this information to my one brief encounter with the Hon. C.J. Lyttelton, later to be Lord Cobham and a famous Governor-General, and I should like to give the example he cited to me in case it is among the Kiplingana that have not yet found their way into print. The Lyttelton family, he told me, had spent their recent summer holiday in a borrowed Welsh castle *(sic)* called Msrw, and Kipling had been one of the guests. One day his hostess had made him play her at tennis, and at the end of the set the following conversation took place. She: 'Splendid! Now we'll have another set.' He: 'But you must be feeling hot, Lady Cobham.' She: 'Nonsense, we're going to have another set.' He:
> 'There was a young girl of Msrw
> Whose statements were often untrue.
>   When asked, "Are you hot?"
>   She replied, "I am not;
> What you see on my face is just dew." '

anything untoward happened at either end it was only too easily apparent. Even as the earnest red head bent over the right hand to ensure its good behaviour something would go wrong in the bass, when it transferred its attention to the left hand something else would go wrong in the treble, and so with gathering momentum it proceeded: the more things went wrong the wronger they continued to go, and the red head turned incessantly this way and that like the head of a spectator at Wimbledon. An encore was ecstatically demanded, and the demoralised pianist obliged us by starting at the point where he had left off and going on from there. We even tried for a second encore, but authority decided that the Roman holiday had lasted long enough.

In the school magazine of April 1923 there was an article on the coming cricket season. It ended with the question, 'But where are we to find a wicket-keeper?' and I said to myself, 'I wonder if just *possibly . . .* '

The possibility had clearly not yet occurred to Mr. Craig, the master in charge of cricket, for when we came back that May I found that I was still only in the second game; but at a quite early point in our short season (short because all the tedious business of the sports and their preliminaries had to be gone through before it could even start) the call unexpectedly came. Mr. Craig had hit on the idea of staging a Liverpool versus Manchester match for the first game, and the nearest known approach to a Mancunian wicket-keeper was myself. It was one of my better days, and as I stood up to the wicket taking ball after ball with quiet assurance I had the deep satisfaction of realising that my chance had at last been given and I was making the most of it. I was aware too that those around me were being duly impressed, though the only remark made to me that I can recall was a cheerful irrelevancy from slip; he was another Bowdon boy who had met Ruth and me at parties, and when I shed a glove to get my handkerchief out of the pocket of my shorts he observed; 'I'm glad to see you don't keep it up your knickers like your sister.'

The opening match was an 'A' eleven match against a small school called Braeside, and I was chosen to play. My innings intensified my superstitious belief that there was something peculiarly dangerous about a first ball, but I kept wicket competently enough to be chosen again for the proper first eleven match that followed. Braeside had warned us that Moreland House, Heswall, had a demon of a fast bowler, and it could have been in this match that we met him. He was indeed frightening: he

32

hurled the ball down from an exceptional height, and you heard it whistle as it passed your bat. But he gave me a chance to show my mettle in a new way. The wickets had been tumbling fast before I went in, but, with a courage I never knew I had, I stood up and kept my bat straight; my four runs were all accidental, but the twenty minutes of my stay enabled my well-set partner to score some badly-needed runs at the other end, and my contribution was duly acknowledged in the July number of The Leasian. All might have been well had the match against Mostyn House, Parkgate, not been played away; for the boundary at one end was reprehensibly short, and no convenient long leg was posted, and by now I had probably become a little complacent anyhow. I was myself inclined to consider my 22 byes a reasonable allowance under the conditions, but as the coach took us back afterwards Mr. Craig disillusioned me by announcing for all to hear, 'Poppy, I think it's time you had a rest.'

I was recalled from exile for the Fathers' Match, perhaps because while I was still in favour my own father had been invited to lead the opposition. I was now of course on my best behaviour, and I let one bye. In the next match I let two byes, and there were only two matches to come. That must surely be that, I thought; I could even be captain next season, as Johnny Monkhouse had been two years before. But I failed to allow for the caprices of Mr. Craig's wayward Irish temper. In the penultimate match my handling was as smooth as ever, but there were two counts on which I could be faulted: I kept forgetting Craig's injunction to lob the ball back to the other end instead of rolling it along the wet grass, and I had developed a passing quirk of the psyche which at least twice inhibited me from removing the bails when the batsman was well out of his ground — I merely rolled the ball back as before, and he must have marvelled to see it repass his stranded feet so amicably. There was a short stoppage for rain in the middle of the innings, and as we sheltered under the trees Craig said to me, 'Take off those pads and hand them over to Clark.' They weren't *those* pads, they were *my* pads; but I had of course to obey his order, aware as I did so that my obedience was a token of abdication, and hoping that people wouldn't notice my face. For the last match I was down as scorer. From that day to this I have never been able to see a man having a bad time of it behind the wicket without thinking, 'Oh dear, I do hope they won't make him take his pads off.'

Yet even that wasn't the end. One afternoon in August the vicar, a cricketer of some repute in those parts, invited me along with two or three other boys to practise in his garden, and his report afterwards was that he thought me highly promising; he had been especially impressed by my back play. When I learnt this my whole retrospective view of the 1923 season was changed: the true balance of success and failure had at last been established, and it was confirmed that the great poet was a very good cricketer as well.

There were only two things that mattered in the school year of 1923 — 4, the Eton scholarship and the cricket season, and for them I had to wait till the summer. I have nothing much to say about the first two terms — the trial run with the Fettes papers in March has already been mentioned — but a little incident that took place that January is possibly worth recording.

Just before I was due to go back to school the word came that somebody who had been at one of the parties to which Ruth and I had gone had contracted an infectious disease; I was therefore in quarantine, and had to stay at home for two or three weeks longer. My mother could help me to keep abreast on Zola's *L'Attaque du Moulin,* but a professional hand was needed for the classics, and Pike Smith's daughter Kate, a good scholar and a good teacher, was called in to give it. She was somewhat disturbed by the gay abandon of some of my grammar, and as we sat together at my father's desk one evening she took it on herself to say, 'I think Eton may be flying rather high;' then as she looked round at me, 'You're blushing, young man.' *Of course* I was blushing; I was containing my feelings as I'd never had to contain them before, and I did very well to wait till I'd politely seen her out before breaking down. When I told my masters of the episode on my return I was relieved to find that they weren't much concerned: after all Eton had been Dealtry's own idea in the first place, and he needed firmer evidence than that before he was prepared to reconsider it.

In May I found myself generally recognised from the start as not only the school wicket-keeper but the one certain opening batsman — which in itself suggested that I might have been allowed the wear of the colours on my sweater through the winter season. I made a thirty and a twenty before that month was over, and on the first Saturday of June I was many miles away: I was spending the afternoon with my mother at the Wembley Exhibition, trying to forget that I had done my last paper at Eton in the morning and that by the time we got to my grandmother's house in Wimbledon there would be a telegram waiting for us on the hall table.

The examination had begun on the Thursday. The first paper was English, and according to my mother's account I came out 'beaming'. Not so after the second paper: it was Mathematics I, and though Mathematics II was mercifully optional, Mathematics I was quite enough for me. My heart sank lower and lower as I read through that paper: question 1, no; question 2, no; question 3, no . . . question 13, no. My very bladder protested in sympathy; but in the vast and ancient Upper School, with the invigilator sitting so far away in front and the lines of venerable white busts gazing down so sternly on me from either wall, I couldn't dream of breaking the silence with a 'Please, sir . . .' It must have taken all my mother's love and skill to rally my resources in time for the next exam, but she managed it somehow, and I got through what remained without any further alarms. But even as we left together at the end of Saturday morning I realised that in the course of those two and half days the issue had come to matter to me in a new way: once I had seen Eton, once I had seen the playing-fields and School Yard with College Chapel and Lupton's Tower and the Founder's statue in the middle, I knew that I could never bear to go anywhere else. The telegram we found six hours later read 'Longson sixth', and I couldn't sleep that night for sheer happiness.

A fortnight after that we played Elleray Park away. It was my first experience of keeping on a fast unwatered pitch, and half-way through their innings a ball rose steeply enough to hit me on the mouth and loosen two front teeth. It was a bad blow to learn that I shouldn't be allowed to keep wicket again that term, for I loved doing it and I had my own personal reason to dislike the idea of being an ordinary fielder; but at least there was no fear of my being ordered to take off my pads for a second time, and my substitute never did quite well enough to suggest any uncomfortable thoughts. It was also the firm hardness of that wicket which permitted me the satisfaction of scoring my maiden fifty, which was worth a whole mouthful of loose teeth. A bare two weeks earlier I had touched the heights of bliss, yet if you were to ask me when was my supreme hour of serene contentment I should see myself standing at a crease which had become pleasantly familiar by now, and noticing that the top line of the distant scoreboard had just moved on to ninety. I was almost at Lord's already.

My performance in the remaining few matches was meagre, but no matter: the next fifty was always just round the corner, or would have been had not our season been so cruelly short. The one disappointment that hurt was my failure in the Fathers' Match, for my own father was again the captain and I had been determined to make the old man proud of me. But there was another cricketer in that team besides my father — his name was by no coincidence MacLaren — and between them those two were my undoing. I scored a single in the opening over, and then MacLaren tested me with the first outswinger I had even seen. Against any of the other sides we met my uppish thick edge would have gone safely for two, but second slip was now E.H. Longson and the ball was within the reach of his right hand. Once again I had to fight down my tears as I disarmed, and I hoped that my bearing was suitably casual as I walked over to my mother's deck-chair. But when I reached her all I could rise to was 'Did you see Daddy, Mummy?' and she didn't do much better: and it was still very early in a long afternoon.

In my last week at The Leas the master on duty was Mr. Hadley, and one night when he had turned out the dormitory lights and closed the door I was driven by some cause unknown to yell out, 'Good night, Doddy!' The door was reopened, and a quiet voice spoke into the darkness. 'At the masters' dinner table the other night we were discussing who was the biggest baby who had ever been in the First Form, and we all agreed that it was you.' The door was closed again, and there was a prolonged silence as we all tried to recover from that shattering pronouncement. My own reaction was one of deep indignation that a boy of such a standing as mine should have been thus humiliated before his peers: it didn't occur to me that masters could have their feelings too and Hadley of all people deserved better than that at my hands, or even that a message had been passed which I might do well to take seriously.

ETON

My first vivid impression of life at Eton was sartorial. My fellows and I had arrived the evening before in the prescribed bowler hats and ordinary suits, but we now appeared in our new school dress, and that dress was not uniform. I suddenly realised that a group of boys roughly the same in age could be inexorably divided into big boys and little boys, and that I, though I had never been aware of the fact at The Leas, was a little boy; of the original thirteen of my election (as each year of Collegers was called[1]) five were already well-set-up young men flaunting tails, whereas I was still to be in jackets up till my second Fourth of June, some weeks after my fifteenth birthday. Worse, the making of my own jackets suit had been entrusted to an Altrincham outfitter, who had done the job in the only way he knew and thereby let me in for a serious crisis: for the wearing of grey trousers without turn-ups was one of the privileges of Pop itself — Pop, the Eton Society, a godlike athletocracy (though the Captain of the School and the Captain of the Oppidans were admitted *ex officio*) whose members strolled through the streets of Eton resplendently attired, with braid round their tail-coats and seals upon their hats, fancy waistcoats, stick-up collars, white butterfly ties, *and* of course grey sponge-bag trousers without turn-ups. For the moment all I could do was to improvise some sort of makeshift turn-ups on the pair I was wearing and dash to my tailors as soon as I could with the other pair, and that done I was left in peace. The trousers themselves for some reason I was allowed to retain; the 1924 election accepted them as a rather pleasant eccentricity, and they came to be tolerantly known as 'the leathers'.

1. The seventy King's Scholars, whose names were officially followed by the initials 'K.S.', lived together in the large building known as College; for most competitive purposes they were divided into College A and College B. The boys in the houses outside were called Oppidans, and the housemasters were called house tutors; an Oppidan would refer to his housemaster as 'm'tutor' and to his house as 'm'tutor's'. The Captain of the School was statutorily the senior Colleger, and Sixth Form consisted of the ten senior Collegers and the ten senior Oppidans.

The second strong impression was that made by Chamber Questions. Throughout the holidays I had been regaling myself with vague but delectable dreams about the citadel of high and ancient traditions which I was shortly to enter; and it came as a rude shock to my hopeful idealism when I learnt that, apart from the normal business of life, my first main task was to prepare myself for a rigorous examination, a fortnight later, in the games colours of the school. The task was a formidable one: for the field game there was School Field, College Field, and the House Colours of twenty six houses, of which some were threefold and one or two involved meaningless words like magenta; for the wall game College Wall, Oppidan Wall, Mixed Wall; for cricket the Eleven, the XXII, 2nd Upper Club, College Cricket, Lower Club, Upper Sixpenny; for rowing the Eight, the Monarch, Upper Boats, Lower Boats; there was also the Rugby XV, Fives Choices, Racquets Choices, and the Shooting VIII. The exercise was, I suppose, necessary; it was all, or most of it at least, information which we should have to acquire some time or other, and the sooner its acquisition was cleared out of the way the better. But the whole thing was done too drastically and too despotically, and the Philistinism of the implied priorities, combined with our austere living conditions and the committed unfriendliness of such as we saw of our immediately senior election (who were presumably doing as they had been done by), gave me in those first few weeks the feeling that this was a very strange world of which I had become a denizen, and I wasn't going to like it much.

Chamber was, with one or two minor qualifications, all that remained for boarding purposes of the original Long Chamber, which had occupied the whole upper storey of the north side of School Yard and housed all the seventy scholars for whom Henry the Sixth, following the good example set at Winchester by William of Wykeham, had built it in the fifteenth century. For the great majority of Collegers more civilised accommodation had since been provided, and Chamber was reserved for the junior fifteen. It was a vast inhospitable edifice divided into 'stalls', or darkly varnished study-cubicles some eight feet high, each with a heavy green curtain to serve as a door and a high Gothic window in the opposite wall. The furniture consisted of a desk with drawers, a single hard chair (which one eventually supplemented with something more comfortable for the entertainment of friends), a bed that spent most of its time shut up in a cupboard, a looking-glass, a wash-basin, a bath-tub hanging on the wall, and a water-can. The basin had one tap only, and to get hot water for your compulsory nightly bath you had to carry the can a long way to the hot tap in Lower Passage. When you had filled your tub you tempered the heat of its contents with the water from your basin, conveyed by a rubber siphon. The line of stalls along the northern wall was broken by an open space containing a huge fireplace, benches on either side, and a large round table in the middle. This was clearly intended to be a general meeting-place for our leisure moments, but I don't remember that we used it much in that way. What I do very well remember was the use to which the *table* was put; for the Captain of Chamber had the right to chastise offenders with his siphon, and it was over that table that the offender had to bend. The commonest charge was that of 'cheek to Senior Election', and it was a charge that the unwary found it very easy to incur.

In our stalls we lived and moved and had our being, and above all we worked; to some extent our life was like that in a monastery, but a liberal kind of monastery in which one monk could drop in on another every now and then, and snatches of conversation could be exchanged from cell to cell. We became quite fond of our stalls as time went on.

Our week-days began with Early School at 7.30, followed by Chapel and by three other periods before the morning was over; on three of the six days there were also two afternoon periods, on two there were ninety minutes of 'private business' with one's classical tutor, and every day there were compulsory games. At 9 p.m. came College prayers, held just below Chamber in a room of which some of the timbers were said to have come from the Armada, and thereafter bath and bed.

The last period of the morning had an interest of its own; for the Head Master held his daily court immediately after it, and there was always a chance of the door being suddenly thrust open to reveal a stern figure wearing the stick-ups and butterfly tie of a Sixth Former, who would demand, 'Is So-and-So in this division, sir?' and on being told yes would announce, 'He is to see the Head Master at a quarter to twelve.' There was a boy of my vintage called Hopwood, who once exploited the known vagueness of his master to absent himself from that period completely, except for the moment at which he appeared, impressively adorned, and asked whether Hopwood was in that division. Directed by the eager 'Yes, sir! Yes, he is!' of the rest of the division, the innocent man gave the required answer; but I doubt if that was where the matter ended for Hopwood.

What I have called the Head Master's court was in fact known as the Bill. The great man sat in his small room in a corner of School Yard, attended by one of the Praepostors, or Sixth Formers on

39

duty for the week. The other Praepostor stood without and took the names of the quiet queue of malefactors, and it always caused a stir when one of them was told, 'Oh! You're to wait to the end': this meant something serious, it might even mean a swishing. With one exception (which I will not recount: it was humdrum stuff) my own experiences of the Bill were all concerned with Tardy Book. If you were late enough and often enough at Early School you were condemned to sign a book in School Office which was firmly closed at 7.15 — first for three days running, then for six, and so on in geometrical progression. I never quite managed twenty four.

We had no form of organised preparation, only a great deal of time at our disposal in which we had somehow or other to get through a vast amount of work. This was particularly oppressive in the first two months of each half, for in them you had your 'extra books' as well (half a book of the Aeneid and a whole book of the Odyssey, to be got up on your own); these were important because the result of the examination on them counted in Trials, the general end-of-half examination by which alone your place in the election was determined, and till they were over you never felt you had a right to any relaxation, you could always be getting on with those extra books. The feeling of pressure was indeed constantly in the air: not only was the society you lived in composed entirely of gifted and highly competitive contemporaries, but you were vaguely aware that the establishment in some degree regarded you as a paid servant, and that the labourer was expected to be worthy of his hire. You might on occasion try to live your life a little more as you would like to live it, but you soon decided that the experiment wasn't worth continuing.

Week-day College Prayers were a simple and perfunctory business, a hymn followed by a few muttered petitions from the Master in College; they were probably much the same as the prayers being simultaneously held in any of the Oppidan houses, though no Master in College was ever known to have exhorted his flock, as a certain house tutor once did, with a testy 'Pray up, can't you?' But no house observed its ceremony in surroundings as venerable as ours, nor did any of them boast the like of our harmonium. As soon as I heard and saw that harmonium being played, I made up my mind that Keeper of the College Harmonium was one of the things I was going to be; and a number of practice hours that should have been devoted to the sonatinas of Clementi were instead spent in learning how to slide smoothly from chord to chord of the English Hymnal without using the sustaining pedal. But it was from our Sunday morning and evening Prayers that I drew my first reassurance that the 'high and ancient traditions' I had looked for were indeed being still kept alive; for the hymns and prayers were all in Latin, and most of the hymns went back centuries further than Henry VI.

About week-day Chapel too there was some slight suggestion of perfunctoriness, for the main business of the day was still to come, but there was much else besides: you could never be wholly unconscious of that long and wonderful building packed with its several hundreds of boys, of the Provost in his stall and the Vice-Provost in his and the Head Master in his. And even on week-days there was the ritual of 'the ram', the slow procession of the twenty members of College and Oppidan Sixth Form, two abreast, from the ante-chapel, under the organ, and into the aisle. As soon as they had passed the stalls of the great the ten Collegers turned aside to the right and were soon in their own places. But the ten Oppidans, now in single file, had many slow paces yet to go before they too could turn aside. They did their best to look dignified, and some, especially those in Pop, to some extent succeeded, but even they must have felt that at the same time they looked just a little silly. In particular the leader of the line, who was by custom its junior member, must have been aware as he strutted that his face was under the keen scrutiny of many interested eyes.

There was no suggestion of perfunctoriness about Sunday morning Chapel. This was the establishment at worship, and the service was nothing less than full matins, including all the morning psalms appointed for the day. The first lesson was read by the Provost, Montague Rhodes James, the embodiment to us of wisdom and greatness; the second by the Vice-Provost, Hugh Macnaghten, an exquisite scholar and poet whose body was found in the Thames in the August of 1930; the preacher was either a visiting divine or a master in orders. All else — the reading of the prayers, the announcement of the hymns — was in the hands of a cleric known as the Conduct; I shall have a little more to say about those hands anon. About half way along the building were the stalls of the Chapel Choir prescribed by the Founder, some thirty boys from the adjoining Choir School and six highly professional men, wearing surplices and the scarlet cassocks of a royal foundation; but in that service their presence was not in fact necessary, for the only singing that counted was that of the congregation — a trifle raucous, cheerfully loud, and when the hymn called for it enthusiastic. This congregational singing could incidentally bring yet a further complication into the life of a youthful Colleger; for this was College Chapel, the senior of the school's two chapels to which only upper boys had the right of entry, and in that mature assembly no one would have had the

41

courage to declare himself as still a mere treble; voices were slower to break in those days than they are now, and many a boy over the years must have gone through a prolonged period of frustration. My own voice was a late breaker even for the times (I was over sixteen when the first signs of any change appeared), but mercifully I soon discovered that a decent compromise between silence and disgrace could be achieved by singing the alto part given in the hymn-book.

Sunday evening Chapel was in more ways than one the grand event of the week: to be late for it was an offence rarely committed, and when Prince Henry of Lubbock's dallied a little too long over tea with his family at the Castle his housemaster had sent a firm letter to the King's secretary, insisting that while His Royal Highness was at the school he must obey the school rules. For most of the year the service was held in electric light, which gave a new splendour to the lines of the perpendicular stone as they rose to the dark vaulted roof, and allowed the colours of the Burne-Jones /Morris tapestry to glow gently above the altar. Instead of the conventional sermon there was an informal talk given by the Head Master; these talks were of a genre invented and perfected by Cyril Alington himself; and they were known, though never in my hearing disparagingly, as his 'bedtime stories'. He must have known what a figure he made, with his handsome white head and his magisterial bearing, on his leisurely way to the pulpit; and as he spoke he must also have known what effect those quiet, rich, beautifully modulated tones were having on his hushed audience. But his sincerity was unquestionable, that was the magic of it: had there been any suspicion that this was merely or even largely an act, he could never have made the deep impression that he habitually did. One of his stories was about a wise man in a village to whom the people used to bring their troubles, and a crucial sentence in their recitals often began with the words 'If only . . .' 'There were many *boys* who came to him with an "If only".'

It was at Sunday evening Chapel that the choir was at last enabled to make its contribution: the evensong was choral even-song, and there was not only an anthem but the canticle settings of Stanford, Parry, Wood and their honoured like. Unfortunately it was not in those years a very good choir; my first memory of Mendelssohn's 'Hear my prayer' is the memory of a hairy youth called Master Mabbott gazing despairingly around him as he laboured through his long stint with a voice that had said good-bye to its prime many moons before. The Precentor of the day, as the organist was strangely called, was Basil Johnson, and he had come from Rugby with an exceptional reputation, well attested by many grateful Rugbeians, of being able to infect a large school with his own great love of music. But in an institution like Eton, where school and choir were completely separate, his gifts had inevitably far less scope: he had only forty-five minutes a week with the Musical Society, and he was obviously not making much of the choristers. It was not till after the arrival of Henry Ley in 1926 that that choir gradually began to sound like the choir it was meant to be.

But I promised to return to the Conduct. It was said that the only qualifications for the post were (1) that its tenant should be in holy orders, and (2) that he should himself have been educated at the school; and in the case of the Reverend Bernard Harvey it was clear that the authorities had required nothing further.[1] He was never allowed near the pulpit, and only in times of emergency was he asked to read a lesson; for his great ambition was to show his critics just what he could do, and given the opportunity he would make his point with disastrous clarity. I came to the school too late to be there on the day when he began a prayer with 'Almighty and everlasting God — oh no', but I did witness two occasions on which his announcement of a hymn was answered by an eloquent silence from the organ loft, and there was a morning not long after my departure when he attained heights that even he had never scaled before, and the response of his congregation was so appreciative that they were kept behind afterwards to be sternly reprimanded by the Head Master with 'The conduct today was deplorable.'

With the exception of tea all our meals were taken in College Hall, a venerable building permeated somehow by an odd smell of yeast; to reach it you had to pass under the mellow dark-red brick of Lupton's Tower and along the Cloisters with their faintly lichened old stone. If you were late for College dinner you had to report to Sixth Form, who would give you the subject of the epigram you were to read to them at their supper that night. Sometime towards the end of the nineteenth century the legendary J. K. Stephen was late on a Shrove Tuesday, the day on which pancakes were the traditional second course, so Shrove Tuesday was the subject set, and that evening J. K. S. read out:

> The Greeks of old observed a meal
> They used to call ἄριστον,

---

1. There are now two proper chaplains with proper qualifications, and though the word Conduct is still part of the Senior Chaplain's full title it has lost whatever stigma it may once have carried.

> But if they lived today, I feel,
> They'd call it   .[1]

At Sunday dinner the Provost himself presided at High Table, flanked by Fellows and other dignitaries, and there was a long Latin grace in which the prayers were declaimed from the far end of Hall by a senior Colleger, and the responses chanted by a small choir behind him. One year the senior Colleger was the Captain of the School, and he was known to believe that the rightful heir to the throne was Prince Ruprecht of Bavaria (who incidentally had commanded one of the German armies against us in the previous decade); the Sunday was therefore bound to come when instead of praying 'pro Georgio Rege nostro' he would pray 'pro Ruperto Rege nostro'. None of us ever heard of any sequel, and it was only some fifty-five years later that I learnt what did happen. The Provost sent for the Captain of the School, he listened to his explanation, he respected his point of conscience, and he had a solution to offer. For the rest of that school year everything went as it always had — only if you listened attentively enough you might notice that the sovereign had temporarily lost his name.

Then there was always the fagging, or more precisely there were always the two quite separate forms that fagging took.

For the first form there was no moral justification: the younger boys stood in no need of being put in their place, while it could have done their seniors no good to be allowed the right of being lazy and selfish at others' expense. At any moment, possibly one when you were badly behind with your work already, once you heard the shout of 'Here!' from the far end of Sixth Form Passage you had to drop whatever you were doing and join in the frantic scamper towards the sounder of the call. You might be sent to a shop far down the High Street or to a boy in one of the more distant houses, and even if the errand was comparatively trivial — even if it meant that you would be actually spoken to by a member of the Eleven — it was still a disruptive nuisance. The chosen slave was not necessarily the last to arrive, but he usually was, and since I was one of the slowest runners in the election and lived in one of the two furthest stalls I was often he. The one thing you did know was that you would never be chosen by your own fagmaster — and that brings me to the other form of fagging.

The fagmaster in College was by tradition a benevolent despot: you did certain jobs for him, and he in return was kind to you. In

1. For any who would like a little elucidation, ἄριστον, was the Greek for 'breakfast' and the neuter for 'best', while παγκάκιστον, in which the γκ was pronounced as *nc*. was the neuter for 'utterly worst'.

theory he was supposed to be some sort of protector, a person in authority to whom you could take your problems, but I never heard of this theory being put to the test of practice; all I know is that he often allowed the use of his own armchair and fire to a fag who wanted to get on with his work away from the distractions of Chamber. And the duties required were remarkably light. A very few messes sometimes demanded eggs and bacon for their tea on half-holidays, but as a rule all you had to do was to make the mere tea, and even in that you took turns with the other fags of the mess. (I imposed an additional duty when I eventually became a fagmaster myself, for I made poor MacPherson appear fully dressed at seven every morning to ensure that I was conscious. But I was a tyrannical exception.) The whole business was also highly civilised; you were always treated with respect and gravely thanked for the little trouble you had taken. The first time I officiated I had already put the pot on the table, received my thanks and closed the door, when a disquieting thought suddenly struck me, and I hurried back to the room. 'Please, Lloyd, had I put any tea-leaves in the pot?' 'No, I'm afraid you hadn't.' The omission was repaired, I was again thanked, and the matter was over. That was the sort of fagmaster R.E. Lloyd was; and I was proud to learn from the Old Etonian address list that he is now a major general.

For one day in the last week of the Michaelmas half the roles were reversed; the fags were now the guests, and their masters went to great pains to provide them with a far more elaborate meal than they had ever asked for themselves. But enlightened though the custom was it must also have been continuously embarrassing to all concerned, and by my own time in Sixth Form a better way had been found. There was now a massed party in College Reading Room; from the start the conversation went easily enough and after tea we played games together, in which fagmasters and fags alike romped with equal enjoyment through such simple pastimes as General Post.

Throughout my time the Master in College was Hugh Kenyon Marsden, a tall lanky man with a dark moustache and a perpetual scowl. By the Oppidans he was known as Bloody Bill, but he was never so spoken of in College; to us he was H.K. His ferocity in school could be real, and even with us his general air of grimness was always faintly menacing. But bit by bit as the years went on our fear of the man gave way to affection; we may or may not have guessed that the constant ill-humour of his manner was partly the protective façade of an invincible shyness, we certainly learnt that underneath it all he was a fundamentally kind man. I had one particular personal revelation, as I shall tell a little later, of just how kind he could be; but even apart from that I look back with wonder at the patience with which he habitually treated me over all those years, for he couldn't have found much to his natural taste in a boy who was not only congenitally 'incompetent' but positively proud of being so. In public too he would just occasionally give a glimpse of his underlying humanity; at the periodic end-of-half festivities he would bestow his valedictory benisons on leaving Collegers, and they were always superlatively phrased and charged with quiet emotion. For the rest he was an unremittingly conscientious Master in College, wholly dedicated to the welfare of his small kingdom; but there was one most unfortunate flaw in his pastoral theory. He sincerely believed that more often than not a good beating was an essential part of a boy's education.

I can't say how far Marsden was to blame for the extent to which corporal punishment was used in the College of the twenties; for Cyril Connolly's recollections are much the same as mine,[1] and his Master in College was J.F. Crace, a gentle scholar who is unlikely to have shared H.K.'s views. All I can say is that there was far too much of it, and that Sixth Form, to whom the executional work was entrusted and who were themselves privileged to beat at will, seemed to be zealous adherents of the policy.

The ceremony was in itself daunting enough. You heard your name called by Senior, one of the two duty-fags of the week, and you followed him downstairs to upper tea-room, where Sixth Form were regally taking their supper. One of them was already standing in front of the fireplace, and there might be a cane in sight — very probably a Pop cane, which had nasty little knobs on it. Your offence was stated and your sentence pronounced, then you were ordered to bend over a small wooden chair, tightly clutching the low rung at its back to ensure the maximal tautness of the skin that mattered. The supreme pain came at the point where the tip of the cane curled round to bite the top of the thigh, and a skilled practitioner could be relied on to make all his seven strokes find the same increasingly susceptible line. As you went out afterwards you were given an ironic 'Good night', which you returned as stoically as you could. But more serious than the physical pain of the

1. My references on this page and the next are not to Connolly's account in *Enemies of Promise*, but rather to that with which he prefaced his review of a book on Eton in *The New Statesman*. Since writing this passage I have learnt from Richard Ollard's masterly *An English Education* that between Connolly's time and mine there was a more liberal interregnum, and I like to think that the 1929-30 Sixth Form, of which I was myself a member under the captaincy of David McKenna, may have been equally enlightened.

moment was the way in which the fear of it could come to permeate your life: you never knew what innocent word or action might not be witnessed and misconstrued by someone in power, to be used within a few hours in evidence against you; any night you might hear the dreaded voice of Senior sounding through the corridors its cry of 'X wanted!' and wonder what on earth you had done this time. I cannot believe that Cyril Connolly and I were the only Collegers of the period to be oppressed in our beatable years by that never wholly absent sense of insecurity and foreboding.

Lent half was potentially a more dangerous half than the other two, for we had to devise our own means of taking exercise, and 'shirking exercise' was something that Marsden could never have condoned; from time to time indeed he was to be seen coming down a small staircase in a remote corner of College after a quiet scrutiny of the names in the squash-court book. But we all of us knew better than to invite a risk of that magnitude, and if ever on his evening rounds he threw out the casual question 'Finding your time hanging a bit heavy these days?' we always had a truthful answer ready. A graver menace, as we learnt when we were old enough, was the charge of 'slacking in Lower College Game', an indulgence we should gladly have allowed ourselves had it been safe, for most of the players were in the 'bully', or scrum, and much of the bully's time was spent in hopelessly dashing, now this way, now that, after the ball with which the half-backs were exchanging carefree kicks over their heads. But we were alive to the danger: as soon as the sly shade of a gowned Sixth Former was descried lurking behind the trees the whisper of 'Spies!' would go round, and we put on a suitable show of energy. I am happy to report that in my memory the spies only caught their man once — me, of course.

I was beaten six times in all, and only once had I deserved it. The beating that caused me the most distress was one of the unjust kind, but the beater had no way of knowing that. On a half-holiday in my third summer David Hedley told me that he was down to score in a house match, and he had been hoping to play tennis. 'Right,' I said; 'you play your tennis, and I'll do the scoring.' That afternoon I duly left my room, score-book in hand, and went out by way of the notice-board to see where I was to go. To my dismay there was no notice there; I had to find the answer by means of trial and error, and since the playing fields of Eton cover many, many acres I was lucky to be able to present myself and my explanation a bare twenty minutes late. What I couldn't know was that at some time between then and four o'clock a more perceptive Colleger would spot the notice lying around and replace it; at least that is what presumably must have happened, though in my more morbid

47

moments I have caught myself wondering whether someone as stupid as I could be might conceivably . . . No; I still see that board even as I saw it then, and there is no notice on it. Anyway, that night I was summoned by the Captain of College Cricket, confronted with the damaging evidence, and accused of telling a deliberate lie. I think he then intended to beat me without further ado; but Fred Coleridge was a just person whose integrity and humanity were to enrich the school for many years to come, and he was obviously impressed by the unexpected urgency of my denial. I was allowed to go, and I concluded that that was the end of the matter. But after Prayers the next night I heard the voice of Ayer K.S. talking in the passage outside my door, and the words were 'Why, what lies has Longson been telling?' I well remember the chilling horror of that moment; it was clear enough what was coming. After all was over I burst into my room and flung myself on the bed in a fit of uncontrollable sobbing; my jealously prized reputation as a truthful boy had gone, and I should never live down the infamy. I brooded deeply over the incident for some days, and at one point I came near to believing that I really had told that lie.

Another point that I have never been able to assess is how far Marsden was responsible for the standard of purity in the College of my day, for at least a contributory part was played by the nature of the Collegers themselves: never once in my seventeen halves was any daring phrase used; so far as I could see nobody even thought of trying it. But even for College my own innocence went unnecessarily far. At one time when I was travelling with my family in a railway compartment I tried to liven things up by throwing in an obscurely intriguing phrase I had met in the Greek lexicon, and the effect was not quite what I had intended; even the newspaper of the stranger in the corner-seat was briefly lowered. At sixteen and four months I asked my mother what it was about the transference of the ring at the marriage service that made it possible for the wife to bear the husband children; my mother realised that she and my father had fallen behind somewhat on the syllabus and she did what she could to repair the omission, but I remained largely unenlightened. I was over eighteen when I first learnt from a Greek poet that there was such a thing in the world as homosexual practice.

The Matron in College of the day was Miss Oughterson, a kind and intensely maternal woman who longed to have children of her own. Once, when I was staying out with influenza during my second half, she quietly opened my door and asked, 'Is my little man in dreamland yet?' Over the last few months I had found myself so often bewildered about where a thirteen-year-old really did stand in the long progress from infant to grown-up that even this sudden relegation to the nursery did not surprise me overmuch; I merely appeased my pride by answering 'Not yet, thank you, Miss Oughterson' with such manly dignity as I could command. In later years I availed myself at least once of her wise and realistic advice, and I was often given the freedom of her grand piano.

Outside College the master I saw most of was naturally my classical tutor, Samuel Gurney Lubbock; it was he who conducted my private business, the reading by a small group of some classical work chosen by himself, and he who corrected my weekly copy of Latin verses. I fancy that he had been a considerable character in his time and won the affection as well as the respect of many of the boys under his charge (the Cazalet family insisted on his spending his retirement in a lodge on their estate); he was a close friend of Monty James, and he had married the brilliant and beautiful pianist Irene Scharrer. I was myself to learn something of his true quality when he and I exchanged a few letters in the fifties, and even at school some suggestion of warmth came into our relationship before the end. But I could see nothing of all this in 1924. By fifty he had become a prematurely old man whose marriage was already falling apart, and all I saw was a well-meaning and industrious master, but joyless and for the most part inaccessible.

As a tutor Lubbock had two great virtues. When he corrected my verses he was not content to do as other tutors did and merely write in the fair copy's answer over any line that he found unsatisfactory; he preferred to take my work away and be able to show me a day or two later how my own ideas could be put to better use. It was from those emendations of Lubbock's that I learnt how a phrase could be made to *bite*. He also never made us do any preparation for our private business; instead he made each of us in turn improvise a quick translation at sight and damn the consequences, which sharpened our wits and steeled our courage at the same time. But alas, deeply though he still loved the poets himself, he had wholly lost any capacity he might once had had of communicating that love to others; all that came across to us in those long sessions, though we couldn't have recognised it then, was the profound sadness that had settled on our tutor's life.

The Sunday private was one of the various roads by which English found its way into an Etonian's education — it was still not an official subject — and with many tutors the experience could be a stimulating one; but here too Lubbock was bedevilled by

49

something in his own self, for he used his Sunday privates to indulge his cherished theory — on which he could never have consulted the evidence of the many expert witnesses he had to hand — that a boy would always 'rise to the challenge of the difficult'. The two works I remember from my first two years were 'Paradise Lost I' and the First Epistle to the Corinthians. In due course I became a devout admirer of Milton, but at thirteen I had to wait till we reached Satan's grand speech of defiance before I could see any merit in Paradise Lost I whatsoever: all the rest was just bad.

Of the other masters I met in those early years the one I recall with the warmest affection was J.H.L. Lambart, who in his quiet benign way must have deeply civilised many lives; to his further credit he saw more in my possibilities than others did, and he even managed to like me. I shall never know how much I have owed to Lambart. The most disappointing was the man to whom I came with the highest intention of adoring him; even if he did teach only mathematics, R.A. Young had toured Australia as an under-graduate and he still batted at No.3 for Sussex in the holidays. Alas, what I found was an ugly man with black hair and moustache and a face like yellow parchment, and without exception he was the dullest and most colourless teacher I was ever up to. Not till I read Richard Martineau's obituary of him long afterwards did I know what a rare and idiosyncratic personality that negative mask concealed: no one could have imagined that on that same M.C.C. tour he had of his own initiative spent a whole night in a dressing-room locker on the chance of surprising a suspected thief, or that once in the holidays he had led a little group of masters into a room in a highland hotel of his acquaintance, loudly remarking as he did so 'There are a number of interesting antiques here', and then on observing the human contents of the room had burst into a high-pitched giggle so disarmingly infectious that the very antiques themselves could not forbear to join in.

Then there was H.E.E. Howson, not one of my own more enthusiastic supporters, but rivalled by few in the craft of lucid and incisive teaching. His services were lost to the school, with those of three other valued masters, on a disastrous Alpine expedition in the early thirties. There was also poor Beaver Badcock, Jovian of voice and beard, but fatally less than Jovian in effectiveness: when a man has once roared 'What in the name of THUNDER are you doing, boy?' and boy has just answered politely 'I'm trying to see if I can get round the room without touching the floor, sir' while still pursuing his experiment, there is little that even the name of thunder can do to help the man further. There was also the mysterious M. Prior, a ruddy-faced master of indeterminable age who came to us with the intriguing reputation of having killed a boy at Rugby. I arrived several minutes late for one school with the explanation that I had forgotten the timetable and gone to the wrong room, which no Colleger in the division could have had any difficulty in believing; but M. Prior was inclined to be sceptical. 'Do you beelieve heem?' he asked the division. '*No,* sir!' shouted my loyal companions. 'He's a terrible liar!' 'No, my friend,' said M. Prior, tapping his nose in reproof; 'you see, they do not beelieve you. Two hundred lines.' The loyal companions saw no reason for further intervention, so once again I was punished for a lie I hadn't told.

And of course there was Piggy Hill.

Matthew Davenport Hill was utterly unlike anybody else in the place: he was *sui generis,* his own man's man if ever there was one. What he meant to the boys of his house we could only guess, though we could imagine that it was something pretty considerable; as it was, all we had to judge him by was what we saw of him in school. You might not have thought that a teacher of biology in the twenties would have much chance of making an impact, but the impact made by Hill was intensive and continuous. He was predictably unpredictable; the tale went that he had once greeted a division with the warning, 'There is a cobra somewhere in this room. But don't worry, it will be quite all right.' His force of personality and his gift of lively exposition made it quite certain that nothing he said went unremembered; to this day, granted a few minutes for revision, I could write a respectable answer on the physiology and life habits of the amoeba proteus or the chlamydomonas. But he was also rather too often impelled to use his talents for the warning of the young, in graphically lurid detail, against the dangers that life might possibly have waiting for them; he would make you look at a slide showing the lungs of a man who had died of tuberculosis, or he would tell you about the hungry traveller who had ignored the fungus on the top of a tin of fruit and wasted away for five years before he died in excruciating pain. One day he urged us against the unwisdom of disregarding any suspicious feelings in the region of the appendix, and sure enough, within twenty four hours there was I in the school doctor's consulting-room. I spent the next two months in the valley of the shadow of death, for my mortal condition had been diagnosed as only rheumatism, and no human aid was now to be hoped for. That oppression was eventually lifted about the middle of the next holidays, when Ruth asked me why I was being so strangely quiet and my answer brought me the relief of her sturdy good sense. But even so I was to develop two further mortal conditions before Piggy Hill had finished with me.

Once I had grown used to it I found College a pleasant place to live in after all; my first year was a happy one, and but for the difficulties that the summer half was bound to bring it would have been a very happy one. The seeds of trouble were of course already there, for in the phrase applied by the late Poet Laureate to his own schoolboy self I was more than somewhat of 'an unsophisticated exhibitionist', and such social success as I enjoyed must always have been precariously poised. By the June of that year Lubbock had become concerned enough by what he was hearing about my behaviour in school to give me a serious talking-to, in which he warned me that buffoonery was at best a pretty cheap way of courting popularity, and that he who resorted to it invariably ended by forfeiting everybody else's respect. But I paid no more heed to these admonitions than I had to the hint thrown to me by Hadley the year before. For the moment I was getting on well enough with those around me, and I had one particularly good friend in David Hedley.

David (though that of course was not what I called him then)[1] had won the top place in the election list of 1924; and though he could not hold it against the more general excellences of David McKenna (I remember how bitterly he wept on first losing it), I fancy that the examiners knew what they were about when they awarded it to him. He had a first-class mind by any standards; he was deeply sensitive, warm-hearted, high-spirited (though he may have had his secret moments of melancholy), a stimulating and lively companion; and fortunately for me he and I were interested in the same things and enjoyed each other's society. The one trouble with David was that he suffered from an unusually exacting conscience. He was himself to prove that conscience's chief victim eventually, for it persuaded him, after what must have been a prolonged agony of heart-searching, into refusing the offered Fellowship of King's, Cambridge, to pursue a course which other idealists of lesser integrity were to bring into disrepute; but well before that it had subjected my own life to two crippling blows from which it took me years to recover. What these episodes were will appear when their time comes, and I cannot imagine that anyone who knew David well would find any difficulty in reducing

1. My use of Christian names in this chapter is largely out of period, and may at times imply a familiarity that never existed.

them to their proper perspective. His friendship with me was destined to be brief, but I shall always be proud to have had it.

In an election far from deficient in personalities — the two Davids, John Cheetham, Christopher Hobhouse, Derek Bateman; I could go on and on — the dominant figure from the start was Edward Ford: nobody else could quite match his genial assurance or his rare maturity. If there was anything that the rest of us didn't know he would be the one who did know: when two gaunt presences appeared in the stalls next to the Provost's in Chapel one Sunday morning it was he who identified them as the Princesses Louise and Victoria; and when some years later a young man staying with the Head Master used our divinity lesson for the exposition of the principles of socialism it was he who told us that the young man was the Honourable Francis Pakenham. He could even override the humiliation of having to make a hurried departure from the schoolroom, followed by an ominous sound as of splashing without; for when we gingerly opened the door at the end of school there were no traces of disaster remaining, and on our return to College we were met by a perfectly recomposed Edward with the explanation. 'Oh, I just went to School Office and told them that a boy had been ill outside Room 23, and would they send someone round to clear it up.' Edward had been born a bare six months before I had, but physically he was a good three years older, and in most respects he could have belonged to a different generation. My regard for him in those youthful days must have been much the same as Pete Denham's regard for Cliff.

By the summer half all our seniors had been absorbed into Lower Passage, and Chamber was left to the 1924 election under the enlightened monarchy of Edward Ford. As I look back on those weeks now I cannot see either that the Captain of Chamber was wanting in authority or that his subjects were anything like restive or badly over-exuberant. A few of us made occasional nuisances of ourselves in minimal ways, and when we did we paid the penalty by siphon. It was all very trivial, and all very innocuous. But trivial and innocuous though it was, it went too far for the establishment. In the eyes of those who mattered we had exceeded the licences proper to those of our lowly station; Chamber was 'getting above itself'; and the principal offenders were Hedley minor and Longson. Sixth Form bided its time.

In the event Sixth Form didn't have to bide long, for Hedley minor and Longson, each in his own way and each quite unnecessarily, both delivered themselves over to the enemy on the same day.

I was College A juniors' wicket-keeper at the time, and someone had told me that the ball would stick better in the gloves if you had first treated them with eucalyptus. The theory as I soon found out was quite fallacious, for whether the ball stays in the gloves or not depends entirely on whether the wicket-keeper has judged it right or not; but I bought myself a bottle of eucalyptus on the strength of it, and David Hedley knew of the purchase. All he would have had in mind, as he secretly introduced those fatal drops into my water-can, was the shock that the sudden upsurge of pungent steam would give me when I poured out the contents; it didn't strike him that the same pungent steam might leave a trail all the way from the tap in Lower Passage to my stall.

I had just turned out my light and got into bed that night when I heard the sound of heavy footsteps approaching at speed. My curtain was flung aside, and there stood the Captain of the School himself, Quintin McGarrel Hogg.

'There's a strange smell of eucalyptus, Longson, and it seems to emanate from your stall. Can you explain it?'

'No, Hogg. It was my eucalyptus, but I don't know anything about it.'

The curtain was swept back into place, and the footsteps receded as far as Edward's stall at the far end of Chamber, where there was a brief colloquy between the two Captains. I failed to notice that the footsteps didn't recede much further.

Edward then announced to us that we were under silence, and ordered me to give my account of the matter. *Quem Deus vult perdere prius dementat:* realising that I had a large and compulsorily silent audience at my command, and fondly believing that audience to be composed entirely of members of Chamber, I saw the order as an opportunity of displaying my rich gifts of comedy. 'Well, it were this 'ow,' I began. 'Ah went to t'oracle at Delphi, and —'

'Who's that talking?'

Again the footsteps were advancing on my stall, even faster this time, and again the curtain was flung aside.

'Was that you talking, Longson?'

'Yes, Hogg.'

'Was it you who put the eucalyptus in the can?'

'No, Hogg, I don't know how it got in the can. But it was my eucalyptus.'

'Very well. I will deal with you tomorrow night.'

Deal with you: we knew that euphemism, and it admitted of no alternative interpretation. For a time, as I lay there, I tried to communicate with the Captain of the School by telepathy, suggesting to his mind the ideas of mercy and lenience and

54

compassion, but the attempt was never more than half-hearted and I soon relinquished it. I heard the chimes from Lupton's Tower more often than usual that night, and David must have done so too, for he knew that his was the other blood they were out to get, and his part in the story would not be hard to detect. He may even have owned up.

Technically the future Lord Chancellor's address to the assembled Chamber on the following evening was not impeccable. It was a mistake to describe us as a lot of little runts, for his own name invited the notion of a simple repartee, and it hardly strengthened the moral substance of his case to warn us against trying to excuse our crimes on the score of any frivolous behaviour we might have observed among our elders and betters — the very possibility of which had never occurred to us before that moment — because there was such a thing as 'the privilege of greatness'. But all in all that high impassioned voice and those white trembling lips had their due effect: we were made aware that this was a grave and momentous occasion, and we had brought it on ourselves; we had all sinned, we had all most grievously sinned; even those of us with the least cause for immediate apprehension stood a little less securely in their shoes. Then the tirade ceased and the voice changed. 'The rest of you may go. Hedley and Longson to stay behind.' We were executed in order of seniority, and as I stood outside that door listening to what was happening to David I dearly wished that the order could have been the other way round.

A few weeks after this I showed David some verse I had just written. It was silly of me to do so at all, for I knew quite well that I had only written it because I wanted to write, not because I had anything to say; it was the proem in fact to a possible major work on a theme as yet unknown; but there were some fine ringing lines in it, and I wanted his commendation of them. Alas, David reacted in the only way he saw possible: he gave me his considered opinion of the verse I had shown him, and what the verdict amounted to was that I was not a poet. In that moment the great poet was annihilated at a blow, and from that day to this I have hardly ever written a line of serious English verse again.

The immediate positive consequence was that my ambitions took a different turn. The great poet might be dead, but the megalomania that had demanded his existence was still very much alive, and a successor had to be found. For a time the vacancy was filled by the great painter, but the credentials of that personage were never easy to specify, and he was replaced within a year by the great composer, who could at least play the piano by ear. I must not however speak too ungenerously of the great painter, for

55

during his short term of office I acquired an interest and a knowledge which were to serve me well for the rest of my life.

Meanwhile, of inevitable course, I was having to come to terms with the cricket.

After a brief trial you were placed, if considered worthy, in the honoured ranks of the Lower Sixpenny 'select', the nursery for potential members of the Eleven which was supervised by a master and given the benefit of expert coaching; otherwise you went into one or another of two parallel sets of humbler games. I was put in the top game of the A-H set, which was disappointing, but not necesarily fatal; I was also from the start the wicket-keeper and one of the regular opening batsmen for the College A junior eleven, which was encouraging so far as it went. Only by slow and painful degrees did certain unwelcome considerations force themselves upon my mind: that possibly the fault lay not in my stars but in myself that I was still an underling; that the defensive skills on which I had plumed myself were not so exceptional as I had supposed, and that, of those who shared them with me, many had better eyes and a wider range of strokes and more strength to hit with. In wicket-keeping too I was coming to realise that I was not quite the accomplished performer I had fancied: any boy used to the assiduously watered square of The Leas could have been excused for finding some difficulty with the new bounce of those sun-baked and sparely grassed wickets, but one with more than my natural endowments would have managed to surmount it somehow. By the time the junior house match season was brought to its end by Lord's[1] I had nevertheless won some mild local esteem in College through the classical orthodoxy of my defence, and I still look back with affection on one of College A's more remarkable scores, which took all of one hour and twenty minutes in the compiling: Hedley *mi.* K.S., 7; Longson K.S., 7 not out; somebody else, 3; somebody else, l; everybody else, 0; byes, 10; total, 28.

I still hadn't wholly accepted the truth by that first Lord's, I still preferred to see myself in the tragic role of the good man unjustly kept down; but even as I sat watching I knew that I should never play there. The general nature of the pattern confronting me was already plain, though luckily for me the details were not. In the Upper Sixpenny of 1926 I found myself no longer in one of the two parallel games next to the top but in the fourth game out of eight; in the Lower Club of 1927 there were only five games, the bottom three having dropped out, so I was now in the fourth game out of five: that was the way the pattern unfolded. After that first year all my summer halves — the Fourth of June with those magical

1. The Eton and Harrow match, which was played at the beginning of each July.

56

evenings when boys and families gathered on Fellows' Eyot to watch in the deepening darkness first the procession of the boats and then that breath-taking display of fireworks, the splendours of Lord's, the sunshine and the trees, everything — were spoilt by the pervasive, slightly resentful feeling of a brave hope turned sour. Once I had left school I found I could play my cricket happily enough at my own level; but never in those surroundings, not with those too reminiscent fields in view and all those coveted caps.

It must have been early in my second year that things in general began to go wrong for me. I became aware that such crude social arts as I boasted had lost their appeal; my companions were growing up, and the comic business was no longer so acceptable: the nemesis of which Lubbock had warned me was now coming to pass, gradually at first, then not so gradually. Meanwhile I was also beginning to notice that all was not well within myself. Slow though my adolescence was in arriving, I was now close enough to it for the neurotic weaknesses that must always have been latent to become increasingly overt; they were beginning in fact to take over my life, and nobody, certainly not myself, knew what was happening. What effects all this had on my behaviour I can't recall, but if I took any steps in the way of reform they clearly didn't go far enough, for that March David Hedley made a last desperate attempt to help me out of the mess I was in. But once again he misread the demands of the moment, and all he did was to push me deeper in. He was trying his very hardest to help me, I have never for an instant doubted that, but the suggestion of finality in his 'You have lost all your friends' was the one thing I needed least; when a man knows already that he is adrift fathoms out of his depth it is little encouragement for him to be told that he is drowning.

I would not wish to make anything too dramatic of the period that was now setting in. Only at one unavoidable point, as will appear later, was I made to feel anything of a declared outcast; I could still frequent the company of my old friends from time to time, and join in their conversation almost as if nothing had happened; but I no longer did so as one exercising the easy rights of an equal, and the room (for we were all out of Chamber by then) was less and less often mine. On the night that I had my first chance of playing the harmonium in Prayers — which went well, thanks to my malpractices with the English Hymnal; the hymn I chose was Handel's setting of 'Rejoice! the Lord is King' — a boy burst in at my door, exclaimed 'Oh! I thought everyone would be here,' and vanished. He had thought as I had hoped, but we were both wrong: everybody wasn't there.

By the May of my second year I had begun to grow, upwards anyway, and even before my ritual assumption of tails on the Fourth of June I had achieved two fifties in juniors, one of them not out; but I no longer expected anything of my destiny in that quarter, and I ended with a dispiriting sequence of low scores. A knowledgeable Oppidan, scanning in my presence the post-Lord's summary of the junior season and perceptibly surprised to see my name there at all, explained to me kindly that my two fifties had been made against the two weakest bowling sides in College A's half of the competition.

With my third year my psychological trouble — of which I promise to speak as rarely as I can — revealed itself in the definite form then known as an inferiority complex. The great composer was still there, bless him, but he never had the self-assurance of his pre-predecessor, and now he was condemned to live in harness with a strange gloomy creature who was becoming increasingly impressed by the evidence that he was no good at anything anyway. This of course created a perfect vicious circle, for the more I felt like that the worse my work became, and the worse my work became the more I felt like that. All of which might not have mattered quite so much had not the first half of that year been the School Certificate half, and School Certificate mattered because it could crucially affect the whole of your subsequent career. The last Trials before we entered on our various specialities were those of the preceding summer half, and normally it was on your performance in that July that your final and permanent place in your election depended: but if by any evil chance you should fail to get your statutory seven credits in School Certificate you would be placed for the rest of your days below all those who had not so failed. In practical terms, you would still be in Fifth Form when some of your contemporaries were in Sixth Form; in yet more practical terms, you would still be beatable when they were empowered to beat.

My own two dangers were Elementary Mathematics and History. About Elementary Mathematics there was little that I could do, but I could have done much more than I did about History. I was up to the most distinguished historian in the school, C.H.K. Marten himself, but his teaching presupposed a reasonable previous acquaintance with the subject, and he was wasted on the likes of me. In the event the mathematical examiner turned out to be charitable but the historical examiner did not, and from being somewhere around the middle of my election I tumbled to fifteenth out of seventeen.

There was one great treasure, however, which that examination and the school system conspired to let me retrieve from the wreckage. Since there were no English lessons as such, the preparation for the Literature part of the English paper was left wholly to the candidate himself; and I have always regarded my private reading of 'L'Allegro', 'Il Penséroso', the 'Nativity Ode' and *Comus* (done during my convalescence from measles) as one of the most rewarding experiences in my Eton education. In time I was able to revise my estimate of *Paradise Lost,* and during my twenties it helped me through many restless nights.

Then there was the Officers' Training Corps, of which I became a member in the following half. No. I shall say nothing about the Officers' Training Corps.

What I recall of my social self in that year is mercifully vague. In school I'm afraid the unsophisticated exhibitionist did still assert himself too much from time to time — to the end of my days I never had him completely under control in school — but I had learnt enough by then to allow him little say in College. I imagine that on the whole I was just rather dim. I had of course to have a confidant on whom to unload my great troubles, and by virtue of his transparent benevolence the obvious victim was old Crow — later to be the highly esteemed Lecturer E.J.P. Raven of Aberdeen University. How many hours Crow spent in patiently listening to those dreary outpourings I should hate to guess; time and again he must have longed to see his door closing behind me, if only to let him get on with the work I was holding up, but never once did he show any signs of it. Good wise old Crow: he was a great friend in need, and I shall not forget his kindness while this machine is to me.

With the approach of that school-year's end a new crisis was beginning to threaten me. Hitherto I had been protected from any too precise definition of my social standing by the fact that we all had tea together in upper tea room; but once our third year was over that protection was going to be withdrawn. From then on tea would be eaten in our own rooms and in self-constituted small messes, and either at the end of the summer half or at the beginning of the next one the dreaded question had to be given an answer: would any mess invite me to join them? And the answer when it came was the answer I had foreseen: no mess did.

In relating what happened in that first week of my fourth year I find myself once more up against the difficulty of assessing or even conjecturing how far the hand of H.K. is to be detected. But whether at his instigation or not Sixth Form had a civilised way of coping with such situations as mine, and after a very few days of feeding in self-pitying isolation I was asked to join a mess after all. Derek Bateman, Howard Sikes, David Thackeray: there cannot have been three more likeable or more generally decent people in the whole of College, and if there was any discomfort in our little quartet it was none of their making. But they must have found their new recruit something of an embarrassment. For one thing we were specialists now, and while they were all mathematicians I was a classic; so that not only did they and I have too little in common, but they must have felt my mere presence a restraining influence on their natural desire to talk shop. Then there was I myself: I was too conscious of being there on some kind of sufferance, I was morbid and introspective, as a companion I was at the lowest ebb of my lifetime; I could have added little to the gaiety of their mess. At all events they decided in July that their duty had been done, and I was given notice; but I couldn't bear the thought of going through all that humiliation once again, and I made my distress so clear that they relented. I like to think that they didn't in the end regret their charity: for by the time I rejoined them in the following September I was a more cheerful and confident person who had found in the holidays that he was still capable of making friends after all, and in my memory I see the mess of that second year as an easier and more harmonious community, with myself able to offer a more positive contribution. David Thackeray passed out of my life when he left school; Howard Sikes was to die soon afterwards; but I still count Derek as one of my friends.

Meanwhile I had also found a new friend in College itself — Bill Mitchell of the election junior to ours. Bill was a sturdy, warm, lively character; we saw people and things very much in the same way, and our senses of humour coincided. I should like to give some idea of the happy gossipings we used to enjoy, but their quality could not be reproduced on paper; it was too esoteric, it depended too much on him being him and me being me. Our friendship was equable and stable from the beginning, and it will end when one of us dies.

For the first of those two years I was living in a room in Lower Passage, from which I could see across Weston's Yard to the archway at its end, and through the archway to School Hall on the far side of the street — a grandiose stone building illuminated at night by the great multiple street-lamp known as Burning Bush, which stood just outside my range of vision. Time and again I must have looked through my window and seen School Hall so illuminated; but one night I saw it, with unfamiliar eyes. I suspect that even at the time there was a part of my mind which knew perfectly well that I was having a game with myself; even I must have realised that stone buildings do not go on fire, and that if they did they would not present exactly the same appearance for hours at a stretch. But once the fantastic idea suggested itself it began to take command; the longer I sat and gazed the more deeply I brooded, and as I did so the possibility gradually became a probability, almost a fact. Then another fantastic idea suggested itself: if there was even a probability of School Hall's being on fire I ought to do something, and the only thing I could do was to tell H.K., who by now would be fast asleep in bed. It was an acute moral crisis, and from my response to it I would learn how much I was worth as a human being: was I man enough to beard the lion in his lair, or should I have to live for ever after with the knowledge that I was a moral coward? At some time between twelve and one I found myself knocking at the dreaded door.

A start, a grunt, and he was wide awake. 'Yes, what is it?' On hearing my answer he said, 'Thank you very much,' and got out of bed without complaint. So we marched along the corridor in silence together, he with his pyjama trousers flapping round his bare long ankles and I, conflict over and common sense belatedly reviving, oppressed by a new guilty suspicion that I had woken him up for nothing whatsoever. At last we reached my room and he was staring in some perplexity out of my window.

'Where's the fire?'

'*There*, sir!'

'Oh *that*! That's only Burning Bush, you needn't worry about *that*.' Then in a gentle voice which few other Collegers could ever have heard, he said, 'You'd better get some sleep'. That was all. The lion returned to his lair, and I hope he slept as well as I did.

For my last eight halves I was in the Head Master's division, which in a less perversely constituted school would have been the Classical Sixth. I had a hard task ahead of me for some time, for there was all the ground lost in that third year to make good, and throughout I had also the slowness of my personal development to contend with. But once again, if I was to get where I wanted I had to win a scholarship, and this was my chosen and long-looked-forward-to speciality; I was prepared to work at it.

Most of the Latin was taken by Alington, who liked to pace up and down his small division room, majestic in his long black cassock. We had known from early years that he was vain, but so far as my impressions went we never found anything else to qualify our general respect and affection for him. He wore rather than paraded his authority; he was always courteous, even to the extent of prefixing our names with a 'Mr'; you could only be put briefly in your place if you interrupted your attention to the work in hand by fondling the little silver poodle that he had brought back from a visit to the Archbishop's Palace in York. He was a stimulating teacher of Latin prose: the first half of the weekly passage would be done communally in school, with him pacing to and fro in our midst, and us, each with his large Lewis and Short dictionary in front of him, vying among ourselves with idiomatic suggestions. He would spur us on with suggestions yet better than ours, and it was his judgment that established the definitive text. I was always disappointed when he showed me the fair copy at the following week's tutorial; he was taking his pieces from *Cambridge Compositions* at the time, and to me the learned scholars of Cambridge never had anything like the authentic Alingtonian fire.

For Greek I just missed sitting under the great C.M. Wells, the man who did so many things so much better than anyone else did, who played for England at Rugby football and captained Cambridge at cricket, and could yet write Greek verses of which his classical colleagues would speak with awe. His successor was the young Richard Martineau, a fastidious and highly gifted scholar with a pleasantly sardonic wit. The wit was in practice too sardonic, for it led us to suspect that 'Mr. M.' didn't care very much for the masterpieces he was reading with us; and it was long afterwards, as a result of his writings in English, that I learnt how deep his literary feelings truly went. I had been impressed for some time by the quality of the valedictory and obituary notices I was seeing in the *Eton College Chronicle* of the fifties and sixties — unconventional, rich in human perceptions, exquisitely yet never too exquisitely worded — and when I at last got to an Old Collegers' Dinner about 1965 I made a point of asking who had been writing those notices, to be told that 'the best of them' were by Richard Martineau. (My informant was David Macindoe, the present Vice-Provost, who was no mean hand at the job himself.) I have used Richard's work already in the course of this chapter, and I should now like to give the end, as I imperfectly remember it, of one of his obituaries: 'On Friday afternoon he was at the funeral of an old friend, and an hour after his return home he was found dead in front of his fire. There are worse deaths, but for some of us the spring is gone out of the year.' After that dinner I wrote to Richard (for we were now good friends) to let him know what I thought of his writing, and he told me in his answer that he found bachelors easier obituary subjects than married men, because 'widows tend to have such odd ideas about what their husbands were like.'

But we were not Richard and Michael at the time of which I am writing; we were Mr.M. and Longson K.S., and for much of that time there was war between the twain. I was working hard throughout, but I saw no reason why I should not enjoy myself as well. Despite the studied decorum of my behaviour in College, there was still within me a monster of a child bursting to be heard, and there was that in Martineau which evoked the monster. Our warfare was largely inconclusive, for if he had one unfair weapon in the right to set lines I had another unfair weapon in the giggling fit. Bill Mitchell described these eruptions to me many years later, and they seem to have been quite something, as they say: there would first be a full minute of silent shudderings and heavings and quakings, while my hand was clamped firmly over my mouth and my face grew steadily redder and redder, and then the hand would break away and out it would come — peal after peal of wild uncontrollable merriment, going on and on and on. It must have been badly disruptive to the work of the division, and very hard on its young master; this was not at all the sort of thing he had had in mind when he accepted that elevated post. Bill loved these occurrences, and found his own ways of inducing them; he well earned the 1000 lines he was once set within a single fortnight.

The classical education we received in the Head Master's Division was open to three serious adverse criticisms: we weren't taught nearly enough ancient history; we were taught nothing of the theory of syntax as prescribed by the Higher Certificate we didn't take, a valuable intellectual discipline which would have stimulated our thinking in a new way and made the dry bones live; worst of all, we were taught nothing about ancient art or architecture. But as a purely literary form of classical education ours must rarely have been bettered. If we didn't know much about how the Greeks and Romans lived their daily lives, we had a pretty fair idea of how they thought and how they could feel. Partly, no doubt, because we were unfettered by the Higher Certificate, we read more widely than the boys at most other schools (Mackail's *Greek Anthology,* for example, was familiar territory); and above all we had the benefit of Eton's traditional insistence, from early youth up, on the primacy of composition in verse. By the time we left we had written in at least five Latin metres and at least three Greek ones, and as a result we were better able to understand and appreciate the poetry we were reading (we got more pleasure out of the jewelled phrases and followed the subtleties of the rhythm more perceptively, we could see why that word had been placed *there* and not *there*), and this led in its turn to a greater understanding and appreciation of Tennyson and Gray and especially Milton; we had the freedom of two choice second vocabularies; we were made to regard our work with something like the eyes of an artist, and if we didn't happen to be exceptionally creative we were brought as near as we could come to being poets.

With every March came the solemn ritual of the Newcastle Scholarship. The names of the year's Scholar and Medallist would in due course be added to the proud list inscribed in gilt lettering on the board in the Head Master's division room, and the award was still a highly considered honour; in the old days when almost everyone read classics the competition must have been formidable indeed. To some extent we resented the Newcastle as an untimely interruption of our normal studies, for in addition to the nine classical papers there were three in divinity: one was on a gospel, to be read in Greek; one was on the Acts of the Apostles, also to be read in Greek; the third was divided between The Bible (*sic*) and a period of church history which varied from year to year. It was this third paper that was the nuisance: The Bible had to look after itself,[1] but the church history required the temporary assimilation of a multitude of intrinsically tedious facts. In 1928 I listened through the long adjudication with the humility of one who never expected to figure noticeably in such high proceedings, but by 1929 I had advanced enough to win a modest place on the Select. That was the year in which the favourite Bernard Burrows was beaten to the post by David Hedley, and I shall have a little more to say about that in a few pages' time.

It may be asked what the great composer was doing all this while. Well, he was placidly getting on with his job, and sucking out thereof no small advantage; but any illusions of greatness were gradually going into eclipse. I never regarded myself as having much originality, I didn't even want to have much: all I tried to do was to produce a little more of the kind of music I liked best. True, it was nothing less than a symphony I was at work on for most of the time, and many and happy were the hours I devoted to it; but I had no expectation of its ever being *performed* anywhere, and I guessed that it would probably end its days as Symphony No.1 in E flat, the 'Unfinished'. I was helped throughout by the advice and encouragement of Dr. Ley, and more importantly I had the privilege of getting to know that loveable and uniquely gifted man.

When Henry George Ley was about nineteen Basil Harwood relinquished the organ of Christ Church Cathedral to enjoy a

---

1. The 1930 Medallist, M.L.Y. Ainsworth, was reputed in College to be reading through the whole of the Authorised Version. Many years later I learnt that the legend had been transferred to myself, and I was suitably indignant: if a man has to be calumniated, he prefers the calumny to be at least in character.

newly inherited legacy, and perhaps for the only time in history an undergraduate was appointed to the post — which faced the establishment with an unprecedented problem. The late C.D. Broad regarded man as occupying a somewhat anomalous position in the divine household in that he was 'too coarse to be allowed in the drawing room, yet too refined to be relegated to the stable', and the authorities of Christ Church seem to have viewed their new organist in much the same light: an undergraduate couldn't dine with the Fellows, yet neither could the Cathedral organist dine with undergraduates. Only one solution was possible; Mr. Ley would have to dine by himself, and a small table was set for his accommodation. But his fellow undergraduates came to his rescue as soon as they could; at the end of dinner (so the legend went) they would rush up to him, seize him, ply him with as much liquor as their purpose required (which I fancy wouldn't have been very much), then drag him up into the Cathedral organ loft to play them 'O ruddier than the cherry' with the full resources of the great instrument's pedal reeds. By the time he came to us he was a plump rubicund little man with twinkling eyes and a deceptive, but not wholly deceptive, air of ingenuousness, and to look at him you would have thought that the playing of a large organ was the last thing he could manage; for nobody with those short arms and that generous paunch should have been able to reach the top keyboard and nobody with one leg so much longer than the other should have had any sure command of the pedals. But he played the organ as few men can have played it before or since.

Of all the organists I have ever heard he was the only one for whose playing 'poetic' suggested itself as the most aptly descriptive word (in Brahms's 'Es ist ein Ros' entsprungen', for instance, he discovered sensitive nuances unrevealed to others), and the only one who made me see visions and dream dreams, at fifty as at seventeen; at Eton he never had a chance to practise, yet day after day he would sail easily through one or another of the big works, always with infallible accuracy and a masterly sense of musical architecture. After Sunday services a devout body of masters and senior boys would always stay behind in the ante-chapel to hear the voluntary out, and if it happened to be a Handelian voluntary the Provost would certainly be standing there in our midst, nodding his wise old head to the music he loved beyond all other. On all ordinary occasions Ley was naturally imperturbable, but exceptional circumstances could undo him utterly: in his single recording for H.M.V. his playing was unrecognisable from the first bar; in the 1937 coronation he made a shattering mistake to which for the rest of his life no one ever referred in his company; and once when

Malcolm Sargent was among the small gathering up in the loft his general performance was so strange that Sargent asked 'What on earth's wrong with you today, Henry?' to receive only the miserable answer, 'I don't know. I think it must be you.' He had the rare distinction of playing in three successive coronations, and that in itself should have won him a knighthood; but because he and his wife Evelyn were so happy at Eton he turned down the offer of two royal appointments, one at St. George's, Windsor, and the other at Westminster Abbey itself, and I suppose your true knight doesn't behave like that.

In 1928 yet another pillar of Lubbock's world collapsed, for a new rule now came into force under which no tutor was allowed to retain his house in the school year following his fifty-sixth birthday. No doubt he still had the same number of pupils, for his successor C.E. Sladden was a scientist and in that respect would have kept him loyally supplied in the four years yet to go, but his tiny pupil room overlooking the High Street was poky and depressing beyond description; he cannot have spent a single second in it without being bitterly aware of this second catastrophe that had come upon his life. It was bad enough even to go in and out of that room.

On College the new regulation had a far happier effect, for with Miss Oughterson's retirement it brought us Lubbock's former dame Miss George, a warm-hearted extrovert whose uninhibited good humour could be relied on to cheer you up if you needed it. She and I were great friends from the beginning, and she even accorded me an admiration of a kind I wasn't used to: 'People always laugh at me,' she once confided, 'when I tell them I think you're so good-looking.' Her one vice was that she was a sublime snob; in the ordinary way even this would have been accepted easily enough as part of the Miss George we knew, but it carried one highly awkward complication.

There was an agreeable tradition at Eton known as 'leaving presents': when you left you gave some memento of yourself to your friends, your dame or Matron in College, and such masters as you thought appropriate; for the first two categories the memento would be a photograph, for the third a book, and very often the present was reciprocated. The custom is beautifully referred to by Bridges:

> O in such prime enjoy your lot,
> And when ye leave regret it not;

With wishing gifts in festal state
Pass ye the angel-sworded gate.

But what leaving present could one conceivably give Miss George? She had on permanent display four photographs, and four only: Prince Henry as a little boy and Prince Henry as a big boy, Prince Leopold of Belgium as a little boy and Prince Leopold of Belgium as a big boy. She must have had whole drawers stuffed with less august likenesses: were you to add yet one more to their unprofitable number? I cannot remember what answer I found to that problem. [1]

Miss George never disclosed her personal feelings as openly as Miss Oughterson had done, but in retrospect one can see that much the same depth of frustration underlay her unfailing affability. Dear, absurdly snobbish, yet utterly loveable Miss George, but for that terrible war you might well have had a son of your own to honour you, even ten or twenty or thirty of them, all happily feasting on your rich maternal skills. As it was you had to content yourself with being a great dame and a great Matron in College.

With the summer half of 1929 my life entered a new phase. I was still only in Fifth Form, as I had been ever since 1924, but I was now a member of Liberty. Liberty consisted of the six senior Collegers below Sixth Form, and they shared most of the Sixth Form privileges: they went bare-headed before lock-up (which the most illustrious Oppidan was not allowed to do), they supped after Prayers in their own tea-room, and most important of all, to me at least, they could not be beaten. The first use I made of this new immunity was to hand over to the Captain of College Cricket the eucalyptus-ridden wicket-keeping gloves which I had been hiding away for four years, and that was the only time I ever heard Edward Ford speak in anger. He did it quite well.

That half I also fulfilled my old ambition of becoming Keeper of

1. Since the above was written ex-King Leopold has died, and starting from his obituary in *The Times* the long overdue restoration of his character has begun. It was always hard for anyone who had seen the later of Miss George's two photographs to believe that that noble figure could have turned out a degenerate son of the famous King Albert; but such was the story given by M. Reynaud of France in 1940, and since a war cannot be kept up unless alliances are kept up too, our own government had to accept it. In fact Leopold continued his resistance as long as he possibly could, remaining loyally with his troops while his government was urging him to return home, and it is arguable that but for his heroic stand the Dunkirk operation might have failed and the war been lost in consequence. The whole affair must have been deeply distressing to Miss George, and wherever she is now I hope she knows that her old idol is at last being vindicated.

College Harmonium. H.K., so they told me, had had some misgivings about my fitness for so responsible a post, but in the event I only let him down once. I had been impressed by a new chant we had had in Chapel that morning (I now know it to have been the badly neglected Walmisley in G), and I decided to use it in Prayers to Psalm XCVII. Marsden duly announced 'Psalm 97', but by some very strange chance I misheard him as announcing 'Psalm 107', and on the principle that the omission of an X should not go uncorrected I boldly interposed: 'No, sir. Psalm 117', a fatal second before I realised that that too was wrong. Even Henry Ley could not have accompanied an Anglican psalm by guesswork alone, and there must have been some relief all round when Thackeray K.S. silently thrust out his own psalter for my enlightenment. Psalm 117 is precisely two verses long.

My cricket meanwhile was enjoying a minor renascence that had begun in the previous season. I had temporarily given up wicket-keeping, which exposed my main weakness; for not only was I slow of foot but my whole attitude to fielding was negatively conditioned by the fear that at any moment I might have to chase after the ball and *throw* it.[1] But I was one of the regular opening batsmen for College A in the official house matches after Lord's, and in the earlier and less important matches, when members of Upper Club and Upper Sixpenny were engaged elsewhere, I opened for College itself. In both 1928 and 1929 I was able to pin up my College Cricket List, but each time there was a line printed between my name and the eleven names above it. I fancy Edward may have felt for me as he drew up the list in that second year, for he had just been a twelfth man himself — at Lord's, when his twin Christopher was bowling for the enemy.

In the following September there were besides myself only three of the 1924 election remaining — David McKenna, who was Captain of the School and Captain of the Boats at the same time, David Hedley and Philip Brownrigg. I was the lowest of the four, but I was the fourth senior boy in the school nevertheless, and I revelled even more than I had expected in the mere fact of being at long last a member of Sixth Form, of daily appearing in a stick-up collar and a butterfly tie instead of one of those sad turned-down things with a flimsy scrap of linen tucked under it. My three seniors asked me to join their mess, but it probably wouldn't have worked, for I had too long been estranged from their company, and as a

1. In 1935 I developed a genuine and permanent trouble in my right shoulder, which allowed me to throw underhand without loss of face. On one memorable afternoon my hand was sticky and I lobbed the ball backwards into the spectators, thereby converting an easy two into a yet easier eight and giving a new meaning to the word overthrow.

failed cricketer eating with three Pops I should once again have been the odd man out; so I was glad to be able, even as I thanked them, to answer that I was happily fixed up already with three friends in our junior election. One of those three, Bill Mitchell, has already given some idea of himself in these pages; a second, Dick Beddington, was a talented historian who shared my interests in literature and cricket, and whose friendship was to accompany me through Oxford days and beyond (it was he who told me only a few years back that my father's name was still remembered in London legal circles); but even were Harry James not dead the other two would agree that he calls for a rather special mention. I have never known anyone else remotely like Henry Percival James: for all his very considerable intelligence, he was as it were 'the pattern laid up in heaven' of the simple soul; you laughed at him, you had to laugh at him, but you loved him, and you never failed to respect him. Sometimes he and I would take our Sunday constitutional together, two venerable figures wearing the sober insignia of College Sixth Form; on one such occasion he discovered a serious deficiency in my knowledge of A.A. Milne, and if the whimsical shade of Thomas Gray happened to be passing near that brook on that dank December afternoon it may have drawn a quiet pleasure from the sight of one begowned senior Colleger initiating another begowned senior Colleger in the mysteries of pooh-sticks.

My main business that half was of course to prepare myself for the scholarship examination at the end of it. My father would naturally have liked me to go to New College, whose cricket eleven he had captained and in whose eight he had rowed, but this year New College was in the third group which held its examination in March, and I couldn't commit my entire fortunes to so precarious a single chance. My choice of Trinity as a college of the December group was made on the advice of Alington himself; he was always a loyal Trinity man, and he sent his old college many a far better Etonian than myself over the years. I had by now done all my three compulsory camps, and an obvious way of adding to my working hours was to resign my well-earned and long-retained rank of private in the O.T.C. I first had to obtain the permission of my two tutors, but there was no great difficulty in that; Marsden said, 'I think it's a very good idea your giving up the Corps. Perfectly obvious you'll never get a stripe,' and Lubbock said, 'I have spoken to Major Hills about your retiring from the Corps, and he was *very* nice about it. He raised *no* objection.' So on all the succeeding Monday afternoons, while my fellows were still out there playing soldiers, I would be sitting snugly in one of the Head Master's armchairs, reading the *Oedipus Coloneus* from the Head

Master's own Jebb edition. But there was something else in those sessions besides the comfort and the poetry and the sense of time well spent, a quality which I could never attempt to define but which I shall always remember with gratitude: Alington was quietly getting on with his own work the while even as I was with mine, yet we still found room for the odd interchange of desultory conversation, enough to let me feel that he and I were somehow coming to know each other rather better as the weeks went on; I wasn't altogether surprised when in answering some trivial letter of mine a few years later he subscribed himself as 'Yours affectionately'. When the scholarship results were published towards the end of December he will have been relieved to see my name on the list, and pleased too, I hope, to note that it had been given pride of place.

That was my happiest half since 1924-5, and the next half — of necessity my last one — was happier still. My social troubles, so far as I knew, could now be regarded as almost wholly outgrown; my holiday experiences, which by then included an exchange of visits with my old hero Edward Ford, had given me further assurance that I was accepted as a reasonable being by the world at large; my mess was as cheerful a company as I could possibly have wished; my future was settled for as far ahead as I thought it worthwhile to look. There remained the Newcastle, with the preparation of a new gospel as well as the Acts and yet another period of detailed Church History, and the Newcastle was important indeed; but my life didn't hang on it. Conceivably, in fact, the issue was of less moment to myself than it was to Lubbock, who once as I left his pupil-room was heard to remark, in the sad tone of voice that was now inveterate with him, 'There goes my one and only hope of a Newcastle Scholar.' My enthusiasm over the Newcastle was also tempered by the feeling that I had no true right to it. Bernard Burrows was of the stature to bring him in later life a high esteem throughout the Diplomatic Service, and as a pure classic he was impressive enough to have already won a first in Honour Mods as a freshman before the 1930 Newcastle was even sat. However brilliant David Hedley's performance may have been in 1929, I shall always believe that the cause of justice would have been better served had Bernard Burrows been the Scholar of that year and David the Scholar of the next; I should have been well contented to be David's Medallist. As it was, if the opportunity was there I had to take it, and Samuel Lubbock's one and only hope came true after all.

On the night before the adjudication I had a triumph of a different kind. I had composed a song — at least I thought I had;

I only discovered belatedly how much the best part owed to Handel — and that song was performed in my last School Concert with the Captain of the School and of the Boats as the singer and myself as the accompanist; it was acclaimed and encored, and since the singer's father was a well-known public figure the event was reported in the *Daily Mail*. By all the known rules the few hours still remaining to me at Eton College, Windsor, should have been roses, roses all the way. But the president of the immortals had not yet finished his sport with Longson K.S.; a career so irregular as mine had been could not be allowed to end quite as simply as that.

As soon as the result of the Newcastle became known H.K. called on me to tell me that there was nothing further for me to hang on for and I might leave at any time I wanted. But I didn't want to leave just yet; I wanted to enjoy the first chance Eton had ever given me of spending the best part of a whole day with nothing whatsoever that I had to do, I wanted to walk about and savour awhile in the one place where it most mattered my freshly-gained if somewhat fortuitous distinction. It was therefore as still a member of the school that I appeared for the last time at the Sixth Form dinner table, my lips already framed for the appropriately modest smile and the appropriately modest disclaimer; and nobody once mentioned the Newcastle.

Only fifty years later did I learn that there had never been any idea of a semi-corporate rebuff, to which my friends had rather unworthily consented; College Sixth Form as a body had wished me well and were glad that I had pulled it off. But the episode should never have been allowed to happen; in the light of the preceding four years there was only one interpretation that I could possibly put on it at the time, and only one kind of memory that I could carry away into the future. On any view it was a strange leaving present to be given by College.

INTERLUDE

In the March of that year I sent a letter to Dealtry, telling him that I should be leaving Eton at the end of the half, and though I couldn't hope for a job at The Leas I should be deeply grateful if he could put me in the way of finding one elsewhere. I got a friendly letter back by return of post: he knew of no vacancy anywhere at the moment, but he would keep a look-out, and if he heard of anything going he would certainly put in a word for me.

In mid-April he wrote to me again. Hadley had been taken seriously ill, and there was no prospect of his ever coming back to The Leas. If I was still free The Leas would be very glad to have the use of my services, and it was for me to choose whether I wished to stay for the whole term or only to help the school out till the new man could come at the end of June. I wished it had not been Hadley that was giving me my opportunity — I had always been fond of him, I should have loved to know him as a colleague, and I was painfully aware that the place would never be the same again without him — but I couldn't help being excited by the thought that yet another dream was coming true. I wrote back at once to say that of course I should be delighted to come; but since I expected that they would probably prefer to have the appointed professional as soon as they could get him I added that the shorter option was the one I was accepting.

I found a very different Leas from the school I had left less than six years before. The ethical tone was as sound as ever, no one could have said that the boys were in any respect pampered; but the sun had been allowed to come out. Barr had by then become a permanent invalid, and Dealtry, though still very much in the school's counsels, had moved into a small house across the road, letting his son Tim take over with a junior partner of his own choosing: Dealtry and Barr had become Dealtry and Wainwright.

Tim Dealtry would never have claimed any inheritance of his father's inspiration, but in his own way he was equally wise: his sense of values was sure, and his clear mind could see and resolve

73

the complications of any problem it had to meet; he was as decisive in action as he was in thought. In his dealing with the boys his touch was light, almost breezy, but he was invariably firm and authoritative as his position demanded. His one weakness was one which nobody would have guessed, and I only found it out myself at a late stage of our long though intermittent friendship: for some perverse reason of his own he resolutely refused to believe that anyone could have any high regard for him as a person, and nothing you said could shake him on the point. His mother had suffered for many years from a false diagnosis, but at least she knew the comfort of relief before the end: Tim suffered in the same way for even longer, and he would not allow himself any such comfort. But his private self-depreciations never seriously impaired the quality of his headmastership, and it can be argued that in the long run they did the school a considerable service, for they more than probably influenced him in his choice of a partner.

M.C. (alias Bunting) Wainwright was the ideal complement not only to the Tim of his own imaginings but to the Tim of reality. If Tim had the ideas Bunting was the man to organise their execution, and he had also certain initial advantages that Tim didn't have: his remarkably good looks and his easy urbanity may well have been decisive in winning over the odd hesitant parent, and among the boys he commanded the admiration due to one who had been a Cambridge running blue and played on the wing for Birkenhead Park. In what I saw of him myself he was always good-tempered and equable, but I should imagine that if ever he felt some show of severity was called for he was impressive; and that if ever he was angry in earnest, he was formidable. He was no fool on human nature, and he knew by instinct and experience how to deal with its aberrations; if a boy had been punished or reprimanded by Wainwright he remembered it because he must have deserved it. Of the two men Wainwright was the easier to like on a first acquaintance, but the longer you knew them both the harder you found it to say which you liked the better, or which you respected the more deeply.

Had I elected to stay for the whole term I should presumably have been given Hadley's time-table as it stood, which would have suited me very well; but as it was I had to take on the time-table devised for my successor, and I didn't emerge from the test with as much credit as I might have wished. I was reasonably competent over the Second Form English; but my other two assignments — *well.* Seventh Form French was the more humiliating, for two of those babies were much cleverer than their master: they convinced me at an early stage that their stupidity called for special consideration, and throughout all my eight weeks, while the rest made at least some pretence of getting on with the job, those two sat contentedly together at the back learning the present tenses of *être* and *avoir*. One of them got a scholarship three years later. Sixth Form Latin was a rather different affair; as the most important of my duties I took it seriously, and I daresay some of them learnt something from me, but I couldn't help feeling that all was not quite as it should be, that the captain ought to have been a little more clearly in charge of his ship. I used to draw two little houses in the bottom corners of the blackboard, the Not Staying In House on the left and the Staying In House on the right, and at the beginning of each period I drew a funny little man in the left-hand house. But the funny little man would never stay at home; he kept popping out for a walk, and time and again I had to slow him down in the last ten minutes of a period to prevent his reaching the Staying In House before the bell went. Once again a warning had been given which an intending schoolmaster would have been wise to heed, if not at the moment then later; but as we know I wasn't very good at heeding warnings.

It isn't for my technical performance anyway that I remember that brief period so vividly, it's because it was one of the happiest periods in the whole of my life. For the first few weeks the mere change of status was in itself beatific enough — you heard the boy's call of 'Sir!', you looked behind you to see where the hidden master was, and you realised that it was you, *you,* who were being so addressed — but though this cause of gratification never quite lost its potency it sooon became merged in a more general sense that all was right and nothing was wrong. I was on the easiest terms with the boys from the first, and that without resorting to any artifice of which Lubbock would not have approved — though if I am to be candid I must confess that my still persisting need of self-reassurance had its say in the story, that one less concerned to please would have been rather less reluctant to let the funny little man reach his destination. Old Dealtry was delighted that his plan was being successful, and he connived at its success himself by using my former nickname in public; whereafter I knew that I had become Poppy once again in my old school, and I felt more at home than ever. Away from The Leas I enjoyed the quiet companionship of my colleagues at the masters' house in Airlie Road; and on my afternoons off I would saunter across the golf-links to see my Aunt Frass, who was the most beautiful woman I knew (Arthur Nowell's portrait of her at the age of three was a Medici Christmas card) and who shared my taste in sentimental music; and often Uncle Kenneth too, who always acknowledged my manhood by opening a bottle of Worthington for me. I happened to be on duty the night before I made way for my successor, and the inhabitants of the Long Dorm held me prisoner while they voiced an appraisal of my general worth with which I should very much have liked to agree; not till Tim himself came in to find out what was going on was I allowed to escape. Eton had something to learn from The Leas in the matter of send-offs.

I was back again two years later, when Tim wanted me to help with the top classics in the July of my long vac. The limited terms of my new employment, qualified further by my own reluctance to forgo my week-end cricket, made it impossible for me to feel that I was once more an integral part of the place; but I had rich compensations in the work I was taking and the privilege of living with the family. I now had the pleasure, as I hadn't had before, of really getting to know Tim's handsome wife Isabel and her son by her dead first husband, John Hood-Daniel; and least forgettably of all I was able to learn what sort of person Tim himself could be in his hours of relaxation.

By the mid-forties Wainwright and Tim had both gone. I attended one Old Boys' Supper around 1950, but I sensed, as I had already heard and was to hear two or three times more over the years, that with the passing of the Dealtry dynasty The Leas had become a fundamentally different place, and I never went again.

At the beginning of July 1930 I was deeply regretting the decision I had taken in April, but as the month went on I became less and less regretful; for my choice had allowed me to learn what low-grade club cricket could be like, and I was finding it good. A few years before that I had scanned with contempt the Third Eleven fixtures on the Bowdon card, and was particularly depressed by the idea of an ''evening match'': never, pray God, should I stoop to so sordid an abasement as that. But it was those very evening matches that opened my eyes. To begin with there was no damning reflection on your personal prowess involved in your being picked for them: anyone not in the First or near it was eligible; that was one possible cause for discomfort out of the way. And even if your pride had indeed been a little dinted it would have still have been worth your while to take part in those games for the simple rightness of spirit in which they were played; the issue of the match was never lost sight of, individual performances were duly noted, but what mattered far and away the most was the fellowship and the fun.

It was also to that July that I owed my first acquaintance with the club's new groundsman, Sandy Bairstow.

Sandy was a grizzled old Yorkshireman with a gnarled weather-beaten face, keen steel-blue eyes, and a thinning thatch of hair that still made sense of his nickname. He had never been his proud county's regular wicket-keeper because he had been the exact contemporary of the illustrious David Hunter, but he had been given his cap nevertheless; for on one of the occasions when he deputised for Hunter he had appeared bare-headed, and Lord Hawke would not allow an impropriety like that. He talked at length and often in the rich Doric of his native Bradford, in which a long A was a long A and a long O was a long O, with never a suggestion of any sullying diphthong to mar the close of either. He had a copious supply of rambling anecdotes, and when he produced one of them we never knew whether we liked them most for the story itself or the idiom and accent or the sheer character of the narrator, for all three elements were inseparably mixed; and sometimes you would leave the pavilion with no clear memory of how a tale had ended but gratefully treasuring some tiny bit that had come somewhere in the course of it, such as 'And Mr. Smith said — yer see they *called* 'im Mr. Smith: that were 'is *name',* or ' "Does tha call thiself a bloody cricketer?" 'e says. "Why, *certainly* ah do," ah says.'

It didn't take me long to discover that Sandy and I were going to be firm friends. He could speak plaintively about me: 'This 'ere Mister Mikil, 'e will keep pullin' ma leg, an' 'e *knows* as 'ow ah don't oonderstand it' — a charge I found incomprehensible in my turn, for his wits were at least as shrewd as my own. He could also be critically perceptive, as when he saw me swinging my bat at an imaginary ball: 'Yon Mister Mikil, there's many 'oondreds of roons 'e's scored in this 'ere pavilion.' But when I returned from a cruise in the April of 1932 the first thing I did was to walk down to the ground and join him as he mowed the grass for the first wicket of the season. 'I shall be twenty one this week-end, Sandy,' I said. 'Oh ay? Tha'lt be a man then . . . The first thing tha doos when tha gets oop is to break an orniment. Then thy moother says, '*Oo brawk this?*' An' *tha* says' — here he drew himself up to his full five foot seven and thumped himself loudly on the chest — '*There's a man in t' 'ouse."* ' On observing his neckwear one evening I suddenly understood why it was that I had searched for my Trinity scarf so vainly; and when on another evening the conversation at the bar turned to pipes and he showed us the one he was smoking with the remark, "I always buy these 'ere bulldogs," I wryly reflected that he hadn't bought that there one, that he hadn't. But I wasn't greatly worried either time; I have always found it easier to accept an established fact about someone I like than to live with the uneasy ups and downs of suspicion.

My father was as devoted an adherent of Sandy as myself. Since he gave up his club captaincy he was content to play on any side to which it pleased the committee to call him, even if that meant he had to play with me; and one Saturday evening we took Sandy home with us to regale my mother with the story of his life. The experiment was an even greater success than we had hoped for; the two fell for each other at sight, and my mother listened enthralled to a narrative containing such revelations as 'Ah buried me father when I were eighteen moonth.'

In 1934 an Australian side was touring England, victoriously as usual, and its feats were being reported for *The Sydney Sun* by that most formidable of all Australian captains, Warwick Armstrong. Armstrong happened to be a friend of an elderly member of the club called Percy Turner; so, of course, he stayed with Percy over the Manchester Test match and, of course, Percy exhibited his mighty guest in the pavilion that Sunday.

To Sandy the event brought a special excitement, and when he got his chance he came straight to the point.

'Mr. Armstrong, might I 'ave a word with thee?'

'Yes, certainly.'

'Doost tha remember that match in nineteen 'oondred between the Australians and Fifteen of Bradford, when yoong Nooton tuke all ten wickets?'

'No. No, I'm afraid I don't.'

'Oh' — in a rather different tone. 'Because tha sees, *ah* were playin' in that match.'

But Sandy wasn't to be cheated of his kudos all that easily. As soon as a drop in the business at the bar allowed him, he stole forth and found his way to a little group who he thought had been out of earshot.

'Ee, it *were* nice of Mr. Armstrong to re-call it. 'E tuke one luke at me, an' "I knaws thee!" 'e says. "Weren't tha playin' in that match when yoong Nootton tuke all ten wickets?" '

I have already wandered rather far from the July of 1930, and the other memory I owe to that month will take me yet further afield.

I was cursorily scanning my father's shelves one day when my eye was caught by three books of *Punch* light verse which he had reviewed for the *Manchester Guardian* in the early nineteen hundreds; one was by Owen Seaman, *Punch's* editor over many years, and the other two by a retired major called John Kendall who wrote under the pseudonym Dum-Dum. Most of their work was in the classical tradition of the day, and I realised at once that here was something that I also might be able to do: I should never emulate the urbanity and broad sweep of Seaman or the fastidious felicities of Kendall, in all probability no line of my making would ever find its way into those august pages, but I could at least give the thing a try. After an apprenticeship of a little less than three years, in the course of which I had received one or two signs of encouragement from Bouverie Street and been twice printed in the *Manchester Guardian,* I made my first appearance in *Punch* a few weeks short of my twenty-second birthday, and after that the rejections were fewer and the acceptances more frequent.

I wasn't yet attempting the ballade, though my future brother-in-law, Niel Pearson, had introduced me to the form when I was still a schoolboy; the rhyme-scheme was dauntingly strict — you could only use three sets of rhymes, one of which had to occur in fourteen of the twenty-eight lines — and I feared that my technical resources wouldn't meet the demand. Early in 1935 I found that I could manage it after all, and my third ballade, written some six months later, brought both the editor E.V. Knox and myself handsome letters from Rudyard Kipling.[1] The ballade, as I soon discovered, had two great advantages. In the first place it was a good friend when nothing that could be honestly described as a theme was in sight: a good refrain, the right key-rhyme, and you were halfway there already. In the second place the very restrictions of the form could help the invention, for the necessity of fitting all fourteen variants of that key-rhyme sometimes suggested a fancy that would never have occurred to you otherwise. Perhaps the sixteenth and seventeenth century composers liked the ground-bass and passacaglia for much the same reason.

My life as an occasional contributor to *Punch* lasted exactly twenty years. Like the Greek and Latin compositions the work gave one who wasn't a poet the satisfaction of sharing in the poet's craft; but it had the additional advantage of being in its own small way creative — the ideas, for what they were worth, were at least your own. At the start I was mainly content to imitate Seaman, as so many of the pre-war verse makers had done, but though I never threw off the old tradition — indeed I increasingly relied on the old iambic metres that suited my immediate purposes best — as my experience and assurance grew I think my work became more and more perceptibly my own; some three years before I was granted the accolade of a signature, one of my Leatherhead colleagues, billeted on the recapture of Tobruk in the quarters just vacated by the retreating German Commandant, was interested to note that

1. See Footnote: Ballade of Domestic Calamity. p.119.

lying on his predecessor's desk was a copy of *Punch* open at a 24-line poem, and when he read the poem he knew at once who had written it. [1] I was always aware, of course, that I was lucky in being allowed to continue an essentially Edwardian tradition for so long, and that some day there might rise up a new Pharaoh who would know not Joseph; I was prepared for the surprise rejection and the private intimation that the personal or domestic subjects I usually wrote about were no longer in favour. But I couldn't foresee that the blow when it fell would be quite so ironically timed.

I was going to call my poem "Forty Two", for it was based on the idea of a second Twenty-Firster, held rather more reflectively than the original one in the light of how the central figure had been making out in the interim. But I couldn't think of publishing it before April 17th 1953, so I just kept it in readiness, nursing it fondly and sprucing it up from time to time, till the vital day should dawn. In the end it dawned some four months too late. I never kept a copy of the poem, but the one stanza I remember will give some notion of its general tone:

> And in your speeches, for the note of praise,
>   The high predictions, the retrebled cheers,
> Let Consolation tune her soothing phrase,
>   And move the table to applausive tears.

I should have liked them to let me see that in print.

In the August of that same 1930, I spent a fortnight with my godfather Cousin Edgar Davies in Florence.

There is nothing exceptional about travelling to the youth of today, but in 1930, especially if your parents weren't rich, the mere experience of going abroad for the first time carried an excitement unlike anything that life had ever had to offer before. To wake in the grey early light and know that the quay against which your boat was gently bumping was foreign territory; to climb into an olive-green railway carriage displaying the messages of 'Do not spit' and 'Do not lean out of the window' in four European languages; to fight your first battle with spaghetti under the eloquent gaze of every diner within eyeshot; to find your schoolboy French unable to bring you a plate of bread and butter at the Gare de Lyons and yet within hours of that see it emerge triumphant from its confrontation with a *douanier ('Qu'est que c'est que ça?' 'C'est un livre.' 'C'est un très grand livre.' 'Oui.' 'Est-il neuf?' 'Non, il n'est*

1. Solomon turned Jehu. p.123.

pas neuf'): all these prosaic and far from out-of-the-way details could carry as much magic as anything told by Odysseus to the Phaeacians.

Then there was my destination: I was not only going abroad but going to Italy, and not only to Italy but to Florence itself.

The Florence of those days was very different from the one I was to find some twenty-five years afterwards, when war and science had inflicted their several devastations. It was a much more peaceful and leisurely place, where you could safely cross the Piazza del Duomo almost at will, and turn into any side-street with no fear of being pursued by a strident Lambretta; instead of the competitive buses there were friendly trams, whose drivers would cheerfully run into one another as a hint that they wanted to get on. In one instance even an improvement has brought its own loss with it; for though the modern electric lighting allows you to see the Riccardi Palace *Journey of the Magi* as the unified whole conceived by Benozzo Gozzoli when he painted it, you no longer have the thrill of watching the gold-leaved colours flash successively into light as the beam of the brazier sweeps along the wall, and of feeling that you too are somehow moving with that opulent cavalcade.

Cousin Edgar was small and neatly made, gentle, courteous, a little prim perhaps, distinguished in essence even if not by achievement. Though far from rich he had always been a generous godparent; for my christening he gave me a silver mug engraved with a relief of St. Michael designed by himself, and thereafter his presents had been widely spaced but always worth waiting for: the Edmund Dulac *Fairy Book,* an inspiring historical work called *The Seven Champions of Christendom,* the lives of great ancients such as Marius and Aristides, and finally a cheque — or whatever you do send a boy of fifteen — handsome enough to buy me the Medici reproduction of Titian's *Bacchus and Ariadne* that still hangs in the study of my Edinburgh flat. He was theoretically an artist, but I fancy that he lived almost entirely on his modest capital; his scholarship was demonstrably frail, for in the Biblioteca Laurenziana he identified the Medici of Michelangelo's statues as the wrong Lorenzo and the wrong Giuliano, and I suspect that the Bramante he pointed out to me on one of our excursions was in fact a Palladio. But he was a well-liked and respected member of the British colony in Florence.

The pattern of the days was usually much the same. I would breakfast in my hotel bed on croissants, clear honey and coffee; I would do my day's stint of the portion of the Odyssey demanded by my new college (I hadn't yet reached the Phaeacians); then I would

81

saunter across the Arno to my godfather's flat in Borgo San Jacopo. We always lunched at the flat (I well remember his relief at my agreeing that his recipe for risotto was far too good to allow the contemplation of our ever eating anything else for the mere sake of variety); we always dined in the Piazza Pubblica, which in those days was the liveliest and most frequented restaurant in Florence; and somehow or other we fitted in the main business of my education. Cousin Edgar was a conscientious *cicerone*: if on the morning when he introduced me to the Brunelleschi interior of S. Lorenzo he failed to take me into the Carmine, or if he took me there and failed to tell me that the frescoes were something rather out of the usual, he was only reflecting a period in which the standing of Masaccio had still be be rediscovered, and I can think of no other major omission which could have been charged against him. Though I cannot claim to have experienced any such 'intoxication' as that wherein Henry James traversed Rome in the times when the square in front of the Lateran was all orchard, I at least felt a deep and continuous contentment in being where I was and seeing what I saw, and probably he too derived a quiet satisfaction from being able to relive his old enthusiasms in the company of a responsive pupil.

One day we went to the Fiesole villa of Percy Lubbock, a brother of my old tutor's and one of the most sensitive users of English prose I have ever come across. He and I discovered a common regard for Bridges, whose 'Testament of Beauty' had appeared in the previous year, and he explained to me that 'the loose Alexandrines' of that poem were a system in which, roughly, the stresses varied but the number of syllables was constant; we also agreed to admire the 'Elegy on a Lady whom Grief for her Betrothed Killed', which I had declaimed in Speeches a few months before and which he had wanted to declaim himself but the authorities of his time had thought it too erotic. Three nights were spent at Siena, from which we drove over in a hired car to visit Lubbock's step-daughter the Marchesa d'Origo at her villa near Montepulciano. I suppose I should be able to record the witty exchanges of the conversation, but all I remember from that idyllic day is that we lunched round a great iridescent fountain, encircled by a low and ancient wall on which basked the one and only green lizard of my life. Just once I made a little expedition of my own, for Cousin Edgar did not join in my pilgrimage to the out-lying church of the Pazzi to see the Perugino Crucifixion there; if he had been with me I shouldn't have worried so much about what I should pay the cabman, and I certainly shouldn't have accepted the solution of the problem found by that worthy himself, which was to smile intransigently and keep the whole of the change.

I only hope I didn't spoil everything at the end. Some perverse element in my conscience had developed a nasty habit of suggesting to my mind possible temptations to which I shouldn't have normally been prone, and then watching my conduct jealously for any signs of my succumbing to them. This evil part of me now insisted that if I let Cousin Edgar know how deeply appreciative I was of all that he had done for me in the last fortnight I should simply be trying to get a bigger tip; and just for this paltry reason, just in the selfish interest of forestalling what would at worst have been a very minor internal discomfort, on the day before I left I lied in my throat and virtually disclaimed any liking for pictures at all. I hope he sensed that there was some tortuous motivation behind this bizarre performance, which he had seen contradicted time and time again by the reactions I had shown over the preceding two weeks; he must also have noticed how eagerly on the last morning I plundered Alinari's for trophies to hang on my walls at Trinity. But I wish that just once in the course of the eleven years Cousin Edgar had still to live I had thought of writing to assure him that his generosity had not in fact been so fruitless as my ungracious little speech had given him to understand — not too specifically, of course, for as it happened the good man had never even thought of anything so worldly as a tip.

OXFORD

As soon as my taxi deposited me at the Trinity Lodge I rushed round into Balliol to see if Dick Beddington had arrived yet. Near the gate there stood a little group of men talking, one of them a former member of my own election who had tired of school a year earlier than most. We had, perforce, gone into the Lord's house together; also perforce, we had played through many a half-hour of squash together; less than a year before, on his one return to Eton, we had strolled amicably together in School Yard. All that was required of him was a non-committal 'Hello'; what was not required was a deprecating lift of the eye-brow and a frigid 'Are you a *member* of this college?' I reassured him that his anxiety was ill-founded and went on with my quest; but Dick was not there, and I came away with the feeling that a freshman was no more than a new boy a little older, and not enough older at that. I needn't have worried; I was never to be given that feeling again.

The Trinity you enter now looks much the same as the one I entered that afternoon, except that the stone has been cleaned in the last year or so. The initial tone is still set by the eighteenth-century stone chapel, with its handsome clock-tower surmounted by four statues allegedly portraying Faith, Hope, Charity and Mathematics, and the orchard that takes up nearly all the front quad; it still seems of little consequence that the rest of the architecture in that quad is later and much inferior, and you wouldn't know that the grass no one may now set foot on was once trodden freely by undergraduates, or that where the new cottages stand next to the porter's lodge had been an old dilapidated building much blessed by nocturnal climbers-in.

The small middle quad into which you pass under the clock-tower, now graced by a raised octagonal lawn, was a forbidding place in those days. Three of the four sides — the dining-hall, the chapel, the back rooms of a wing of the garden quad — were in themselves architecturally unimpeachable; yet they were all dominated by that sinister fourth side. The two dons who lived there were the greatly respected historian J.R.H. Weaver, later to be President of the college, and the wise and urbane chaplain and philosopher Kenneth Kirk, later to be the Bishop of Oxford; but the block still seemed to house the spirit of the Victorian Latinist Robertson Ellis, who might have been the model for Yeats's poem on editors of Catullus, and was misanthropic enough to answer the worthy T.H. Green's invitation to dine at Balliol high table with a letter which even called upon a minor illogicality to intensify its rudeness: 'Dear Green, I do not think I will dine with you on Monday. It is not so much the food I object to, it is the company'.

The garden quad that you finally reach — and as you emerge into it the entrance you see facing you is the entrance to *my* stair, the two top-storey windows to its right are *my* windows — is still, as it had to be, its old benign and splendid self. It was built, so we were told, on a modified version of a plan by Christopher Wren, and from the windows of the central block, reserved in my time for the more opulent commoners, you can look past the period gateway and railings to the whole sweep of those beautifully-kept lawns on which a tortoise of untold antiquity used insatiably to feed. On the first floor of my stair lived the shy and kindly Junior Dean Robert Hall, now Lord Roberthall, and the Reverend Mark Patterson, of whom it was said that to spare himself the trouble of continual replenishment he would pour out ten glasses of port before he sat down; it was also said that under the tutelage of himself and Weaver no Trinity man had been exposed to the danger of a First in History since the war, though one suspects that the story was less than fair to Weaver. On the adjoining staircase were the rooms of the philosopher Henry Price, and opposite them the Bursar Philip Landon held his court, but unless you were a blue or something like it you did better to keep away. There were three such patrons of successful athleticism in Oxford then, of whom the most famous was Brasenose's W.T.S. Stallybrass, widely known as Sonners in commemoration of his pre-war name of Sonnenschein. The mother of a Brasenose rowing blue in my time, demoralised by her son's repeated insistence that whatever she did when she met the great man she mustn't breathe that long repudiated trisyllable, was reduced at the moment of crisis to saying, 'I've heard so much about you, Dr. Stellenbosch.'

On the evening of the day I arrived all the freshmen were given a little talk on seemly behaviour by the Dean, Thomas Farrant Higham. This address was always the same, and the ancient historian Ronald Syme used to refer to it mischievously as ' the Dean *De Moribus*'. The only bit I remember is that in which we were warned against imitating such as 'sought by eccentricity of dress to claim a distinction to which their personal attainments did not entitle them'.

The next morning also belonged to Higham, for he was the Classical Honour Moderations tutor as well as the Dean, and he now held a mass tutorial for all his new pupils. Before I came up I had been told by my cousin Paddy Monkhouse that the Mods man Higham was 'no good', and I have since had reason to believe that that was the general view of Paddy's contemporaries; but within three minutes of the tutorial's starting I knew that even if the condemnation had once been valid it was now valid no longer. Higham's main them was the textual criticism which from then on was going to be a major part of our studies, and the point he particularly stressed was its value as a stimulant and test of literary taste. As an example he gave us an anonymous emendation of the passage in 'Lycidas',

> To lie with Amaryllis in the shade,
> And with the tangles of Neara's hair.

He showed us that the two 'with' phrases were prohibitively ill-balanced, and that such a feeble beginning as 'And with the' was out of accord with Milton's general prosody. Whether 'withe' is the true reading or not, I have never since then been able to believe that second 'with'. And I think I know what the emender's name was.

At nineteen and a half I must in point of simple age have been one of the oldest members of my year, but in most respects I was as young as any of us; if I spoke and mostly even thought of myself as a man I was still pathetically far from being one. My behaviour was very often remarkably silly, but one lesson I had learnt was how to be silly without irritating people; if they laughed at me now, which they did, it was because there was a streak of the ridiculous somewhere in my nature and not because I was playing the conscious clown. (I might have been shaken out of this mood of recollective complacency by an encounter I recently had at a Trinity Society Week-end, for without any kind of warning this man suddenly asked me, 'Do you remember Mike Longson? *He* was *quite* mad.' But the effect was if anything reassuring, for his tone was indulgent; it implied that Trinity had always respected its members' rights to their little personal foibles, and that if my own had taken the form of total insanity it had been condoned.) Physically too I was still taking my time to grow up. When some two months before my twenty-first birthday I rashly mentioned the moustache that I was trying to encourage, the immediate response was 'Puzzle: find the moustache!' I replied with dignity that if it didn't come off it would come off, which two days later it did. But as well as being retarded my development seems to have been in a sense also arrested; at some point or over some period in the preceding six years something definite and specific must have gone wrong with it, so that the bone and thews I seemed to be merely slow in growing were to a great extent never to be grown at all. Even as I sit writing here my aspect is that of an elderly adolescent, and the result of this dispensable complication at a time when one's visual presence counted rather more than one admitted — it would have been nice to command the admiration of Somerville, after all — was that I cut an even more unimpressive figure than I need have done.

At the beginning I was naturally concerned about whether I should make friends or not, but once again I needn't have worried; the difficulty of making friends in that Trinity was as illusory as the ignominy of fresherhood. My greatest friend, then as now, was Patrick Arthur Macrory — Robert Thompson and Edward Bischoff came pretty close, but neither of them accompanied me to 8 Banbury Road or to 174 Abingdon Road after that. I was the senior scholar of our classical five and he only the minor scholar, but I hadn't known him a fortnight before I saw clearly which of the two of us would be the more successful man. He was a full colonel when I was a corporal; after his promising start at the bar had been fatally disrupted by the war (for you can hardly pick up as a junior again as a married man of thirty-six), he first tried his hand at parliamentary drafting and then was only saved by an uncooperative liner from taking up the duties of a Crown Counsel in Kenya, whereafter he eschewed all such false lights and graduated from advising the chairman of Unilever's to being the company's secretary and eventually a director on its board; he was given a knighthood for his chairing of a committee on the local administration of Ulster whose recommendations were only nullified because they presupposed the continuance of a parliament in Stormont; and his masterly and fascinating account of the first Afghan war in *Signal Catastrophe* may well have given George Macdonald Fraser's young Flashman one of the fillips needed to start him on his triumphant career. As a friend Pat was as equable as Bill Mitchell had been before him, and if I were to protest that he was a shade avuncular on occasion he would answer that there are some people in this world who need a little judicious uncling from time to time. He was only not to be trusted when telling a story about myself, for the mere theme would kindle in him a flame of improvisatory extravagance which was well beyond his normal range, and truth did not prevail.

Had I but space enough and time I would gladly dilate on other of my friends, and not only those in my own college. As it is I must restrict myself to doing some sort of justice to Mike Peacock of Brasenose, not, I hope, because he twice played in the Oxford pack at Twickenham, nor because he was exceptionally handsome (he could have been described as a bigger and tougher Michael Dennison), but because circumstances allowed our friendship to blossom further right into the late thirties, and above all because he was the best teller of tales in the university. I never found out whether the story would spring out of his head like Pallas out of Zeus's, gorgeously panoplied from the start, or whether he gave it long hours of polishing and repolishing before he decided that it was ready for use; all I know is that by the time it did come out it was always perfect. The trouble was that once it was perfect it was unalterable, so that he must have wondered every now and then just what stories he had told to whom; if but one of the company was listening to a twice-told tale then to one pair of ears he was in some degree undoing his own magic. My own favourite story was the one about the early morning expedition in the Alps. There were six of them on that rope, all wearing three pairs of trousers against the extreme cold, and the leader was a Swiss guide. At one point Mike decided that there was a thing that he needed to do, so he made the party halt while he fumbled with the fly-button of the outermost pair. *'Non, non!'* shouted the guide. *'Dans le pantelon, monsieur!'* 'So *dans le pantelon* it was,' Mike recounted. 'After a bit it came to the surface; it froze; it jangled as I walked; it was like a chandelier worn as a sporran.' We saw no special significance at the time in the fact that Mike was a member of the Oxford University Air Squadron; but the point was made clearly enough in June 1940.

But I mustn't let even Mike Peacock keep me too long from my own Trinity, for the debt I owe my college deserves a tribute at least as eloquent as that which Belloc paid to Balliol. The sense of general well-being was never absent from our Trinity; you could feel it in all the easy exchanges of the quad, and often you could hear it in the very air; for as likely as not someone would have a gramophone on somewhere, and there were good tunes around in those days, 'The First Week-end in June', 'Those Little White Lies', 'Night and Day'. I daresay, and I fondly hope, that to a great extent the like can still be said of the college, but the pressures of a hardening world have inevitably brought their losses; there is no longer any room for the genial soul who was never much concerned about what sort of degree he was going to get, and the athlete, whose wit and affability used to flower so luxuriantly in the old soil of long assurance, is now far scarcer and has lost some of the standing that helped to make him what he was. It must be admitted that we took the advantages of privilege very much for granted, but then people so placed have usually done that; and if on a superficial view we may have seemed more open than most to the charge laid against Oxford and Cambridge in Lawrence's devastating poem — for indeed we were, *you knew* we were, superior — our superiority was not in fact of the kind he found so insufferable; it was a simple and essentially harmless thing, there was no arrogance in it, and it never went very deep. And even if we were an over-exclusive community the exclusiveness was none of our devising; the responsibility for that lay with our President, the Reverend H.E.D. Blakiston.

There was no denying that Blinks was a snob; he was a supreme snob. When the list of the next year's freshmen appeared outside the porter's lodge in June we always found a quiet amusement in noting how small a number of schools had been considered worthy of inclusion — though certain qualifications could be made in the case of scholars, especially science scholars. At a time when more liberal ideas had begun to infiltrate the university — A D. Lindsay of Balliol was said to have set the lead — the colour bar in Trinity was still absolute, and even the most irreproachably pigmented of foreigners were viewed with mistrust; some ten years before my day an American was told at his first interview that his compatriots were admitted at the rate of one every four years — '*and no Indians*,' the President firmly added.[1] He was an eccentric as well as a snob; his manner was that of an old woman, and he was so pitifully shy that the keeping up of an ordinary conversation was usually beyond his powers; his occasional essays in entertainment were dreaded. But he was not a man to be laughed away. He was as shrewdly aware as anyone in the college of what was going on in it, and in his practical dealings he always knew well what he was about; when a man trying to engineer the admission of his nephew wrote to request a personal interview the answer he received was, 'Dear Sir X, If you have something to tell me about your nephew which you are unwilling to commit to paper I shall be glad to see you at five o'clock on Monday January 21st.'[2] And for all his oddity and narrowness he had his own kind of wisdom — as I hope to show later.

---

1. and 2. I heard both these stories told from high table at dinners of the Trinity Society, the first by the quondam American undergraduate, L.B. Warren, himself. I have since found them both in T.F. Higham's superlative *H.E.D. Blakiston: An Appreciation,* and his version of the second is very differently worded from that given above. But I tell the tale that I heard told; I like it better, anyway. Higham also quotes examples of Blakiston's wit, but that was something never revealed to undergraduates.

The day would always open with the appearance of the scout bearing your shaving-water, for the water in the ewer which stood in the basin was cold. My own scout was a strange taciturn near-man called Frost; he was never perceptibly drunk at that hour, but he often was at other times of the day, and it wasn't hard to guess his method of pursuing his hobby economically. If I ordered a dozen pint bottles of beer he would always faithfully bring the dozen, but the next time I looked in the cupboard there would be only ten; when there should have been six left there would be four; and so on it went. His principle was not unlike that of a schoolboy robbing birds' nests, who stills his conscience by the supposition that any creature so stupid as a bird cannot conceivably have the mathematical skill to distinguish two from one; but whereas the boy's theory could never have been subjected to any empirical test, Frost might have claimed that his initial theft had in itself constituted a valid experiment, that if I had not had the courage to challenge him then I could be relied on never to challenge him thereafter. In this his reasoning was sound enough, but the day was coming when he was to make a fatal miscalculation. At some time in the course of my second vac the Junior Dean had invited some friends to luncheon, and however tolerant a Junior Dean may be he still has his pride; he would prefer his manservant to come in looking reasonably sober, and if that was too much to ask he would at least expect him not to cut his hand on the premises and bleed all over the linen tablecloth. Frost was succeeded by Beadle, a young man of about thirty; there were few people in Trinity whom I liked better than him, and if I was sometimes a little over-familiar he was never over-familiar in return: the master-servant conventions were recognised by both of us as not being of great importance, but he still respected them. I think he was almost as sorry as I was when the time came for me to leave college.

My mornings were, of course, devoted to lectures, and it occurs to me to marvel now, even if I didn't marvel then, at the phenomenon of the highly intelligent man who called himself a lecturer, and in all good faith took good money on the understanding that he was indeed such, without having the remotest conception of how to lecture. The supreme example was the brilliant J.G. Barrington-Ward, who knew so much about the intricacies of Athenian civil law that he couldn't wait to expound them in all their copious detail to the eager students in front of him, with the result that he would be well into sentence three while you were still desperately trying to write down in some form of improvised shorthand what you thought he might have said in sentence one. In direct contrast to him stood our own Thomas

Higham, who delivered his scrupulously prepared scripts at dictation speed and changed his voice when he came to one of his illuminating *obiter dicta*; Gilbert Murray made himself memorable by reading Greek with a soft inflection which echoed his deep love of the language and matched the limpidity of his English prose; but of all the lecturers I sat under that first year the most impressive was Higham's old pupil John Christie, for the literary and technical problems of the *Oedipus Tyrannus* are many and complex, yet he made sure that we clearly understood every one of them. Then there is one figure who transcends this petty differentiation between good and bad, for he insists on being mentioned by the sheer right of having been the person he was — the Public Orator of the period, A.B. Poynton. Mind you, I think he had every intention of establishing himself as one of the great Oxford eccentrics; had he had no such purpose he wouldn't have watched the cricket in the Parks invariably wearing a bowler hat and a bright yellow macintosh; nor when told as Dean of University that a suspicious foreigner had been seen lurking in the college would he have seen fit to warn his undergraduates against the possible danger by putting up the simple notice, ' *Cavete furem peregrinum.*' As a lecturer he was alleged to discourage the attendance of women by making a point of saying something outrageous in his first lecture of each term; but my memory won't tell me whether that happened in the October of 1930 or not. All I can remember is that his whole act (for act it undoubtedly was) was that of a black-moustached, rubicund and probably bibulous comedian in the rich tradition of George Robey; how well his line of patter would have compared with that great master's can only be guessed, for even when it was audible it was too esoteric for comprehension, but he himself chuckled hugely at it throughout, and we all laughed sympathetically with him because we thought him a dear old boy and were happy to see him enjoying himself so much. I can't say what the lectures were about.

The winter afternoons posed something of a problem, for I had been brought up to believe that I ought to take some kind of exercise every day. I was no use at soccer, and my two Lent halves of rugger at school, undergone to please my father, had led me to suspect that there were few forms of slavery worse than that of being a bad forward. I therefore chose hockey. This would have been quite a sensible decision in itself, only I forgot the whole point was the taking of exercise and needlessly told the hockey secretary that I had once had pretensions as a goalkeeper; and as it happened not only was he looking for a new goalkeeper to take over when the regular man went down, but the regular man himself had a habit of being unavailable. My first appearance with the college eleven made it quite plain that those former pretensions could never have had much validity, but Douglas Gairdner was a persevering young man; time and time again the lunch-time peace of the quad would be shattered by his voice calling my name, and I knew that I had to go through my ignominious paces once more. The climax came about half-term; Magdalen College School away, that was the match, and it coincided with the long-delayed return to the side of its captain, one of those large over-serious athletes known in Oxford as 'heavies', who had never seen me in action before. I tried, I swear I tried; it was not through any want of attention that the ball went so often into that net; it just kept on doing it. But it was the last goal of all — the fifteenth I think — which determined the course of history. The ball was struck from well outside the circle, and I decided that masterly inactivity was the line to take; for either it would go into the net, in which case the goal wouldn't count, or it would go out, in which case there would be a bully-off. What I didn't allow for was the possibility of its hitting the post and bouncing back to a point within the circle from which an agile young forward could flick it in at his leisure. At that the heavy captain broke his long silence, and if the three hundred school-boys thronging the touch-line hadn't been gloating already they would have gloated to hear those trenchant words. Thereafter I took to having my lunch with Eddie Bischoff, who lived in rooms tucked away at the back of the quad whither no secretarial voice could penetrate; but I fancy that the captain would have taken independent steps to ensure my future immunity.

I was never to find out why that official goalkeeper was so persistently elusive. It was certainly not because he was working at his Greats, for the one small legend that he left behind him makes it clear that he took his scholastic duties as lightly as he took his athletic ones. It was a standing principle of the 'viva', as the final oral examination was called, that no question should be put with the express design of catching a candidate out; but when my goalkeeper's knowledge of Greek history was being tested one of the inquisitorial trio became so impatient of his colleagues' plain stupidity that he asked the young man what the Spartan general Brasidas, who was killed in 424 B.C., had thought of the Peace of Nicias, which was signed in 421. 'Well, he didn't think much of it', replied my man stoutly. 'No, alas!' said the grateful examiner, 'for he was with God.'

The rest of the day was mine, to be divided between business and pleasure as I chose, except that once a week (or was it twice?)

I had an hour's tutorial with Tommy Higham between tea and dinner.

Even if Tommy had still had to prove his excellence as a tutor he would have proved it in the course of my first two years; for against the full embattled might of the other colleges - and Balliol alone could enter a Duncan Wilson and a Twisteton-Wykeham-Fiennes — my friends Frederick Wells and Hal Summers bore off between them nearly all the honours that Oxford classics had to offer: Frederick won the Hertford twice and the Craven and Ireland in between, and Hal was once the *proxime accessit* and once the number three. That they were two exceptionally gifted men was confirmed by their subsequent careers; for Frederick became predictably a well-esteemed Mods don in University who might have gone further still but for his untimely death in his early forties, while Hal was for many years a leading civil servant who as a pastime wrote some of the best modern poetry I know — accessible, humane, as delicately observant as a good etching, and always beautifully shaped. But both of them would have generously admitted their indebtedness to Tommy. If the potter needs the clay the clay also needs the potter, and the skill and conscientiousness of Tommy's craftmanship can be illustrated by one detail: when we sat the scholarship exam of December 1930, in the three hours of the Latin verse paper Frederick had only been able to squeeze out four lines ('but them golden', Tommy told me), yet within eighteen months of that he was able to meet all the demands of the Hertford. As the senior scholar of the year I protected the dignity of my office by allowing it to be seen that I was somewhat less dedicated than my brilliant juniors; but in a smaller way I too was to pay practical tribute to Tommy's high professionalism, for according to Bowra I wrote the best Latin hexameters of my year's Mods, and I couldn't have done that without the help of continuously expert tuition.

If there is one thing rather than another for which I have never ceased to be grateful to Oxford it is that series of tutorials with Tommy. I came to him with a reasonable technical equipment and a reasonably well developed sense of style, slightly flawed by a schoolboyish over-concern with the impressive word and the recondite idiom; but he soon corrected that. Everything I wrote had to be as good stylistically as I could make it, for that was one of the basic rules, and if an impressive word or a recondite idiom contributed to the required effect it was allowed its place; but the one thing that counted most of all was the faithful and precise rendering of the sense of the original, which meant not only the expression of the thought but also the reflection of the feeling implied in it. I was fascinated by the various ways in which these principles were followed in the fair copies he used, and not least in those written by himself; for he was a fastidious and exquisite composer, who had won the Gaisford Greek Verse Prize in his day by turning the whole of Meredith's 'Love in the Valley' into authentically Theocritean hexameters. It was also he who introduced me to the civilised custom the ancient poets had of quoting from each other by way of compliment, and he infected me with his own interest in their occasional refinement of the convention by giving the quotation an unexpected twist — as when Virgil applied Ennius' phrase describing the march of Hannibal's elephants to a sortie of a swarm of bees.[1] I rarely left one of those tutorials without a deep sense of enrichment.

We were always made welcome at Tommy's house in Northmoor Road, and we soon learnt that his wife Betty (though none of us ever called her that) was one of the most remarkable characters in Oxford. Her unfailing vivacity, her trenchant humour and her forthright common-sense always did us good, and we loved her on the strength of them; we would not have had her different. But it was impossible to avoid seeing that she was too much for our gentle Tommy; he would do his best to assert a comparable if quieter authority, but the effect was never convincing. Proud and fond of

---

1. Since then I have made my own small private collection of quotations with twists, which I hope will be thought worth my appending.

(1) From Dryden's translation of the *Aeneid:*
       And the long glories of majestic Rome.

     From Tennyson's *Morte d'Arthur* and *Idylls of the King:*
       And on a sudden, lo, the level lake,
       And the long glories of the winter moon.

(2) From Pope's prologue to Addison's *Cato:*
       When Cato gives his little senate laws,
       What bosom beats not in his country's cause?

     From Pope's later description of a certain 'Atticus':
       Like Cato, give his little senate laws,
       And sit attentive to his own applause.

(3) Pope on Queen Anne at Hampton:
       Where thou, great Anna! whom three realms obey,
       Dost sometimes counsel take, and sometimes tea.

     G.H. Vallins on Winston Churchill at Westminster:
       Where thou, of mighty Marlborough's line begot,
       Dost sometimes counsel take, and sometimes not.

(4) Motley on William the Silent:
       As long as he lived he was the guiding star of a brave nation,
          and when he died the little children cried in the streets.

     Auden on Hitler:
       When he laughed respectable senators burst with laughter,
       And when he cried the little children died in the streets.

her though he unquestionably was, his own sensitive personality might have fulfilled itself better could he have been seen by his pupils as being master in his own household.

Towards the end of the 1960's I was summoned to a symposium of senior classics masters at Corpus, and since the engagement was for a Friday I gave myself long leave of absence and invited myself to lunch with Tommy on the following day. I had been warned that he had been recently widowered and might need careful handling; but rarely can a warning have been wider of the mark. The Tommy who opened the door to me was a Tommy I had never known; he radiated self-confidence, the slight tremor had gone out of his voice, his friendliness was more spontaneous, he even looked bigger; and it didn't take me long to discover that a major cause of the metamorphosis was the presence of a motherly *Italiana* called Mrs Fellowes, who had tended Mrs Tommy in her last illness and was now willingly staying on to housekeep for the widower. In the course of the afternoon he was called away to answer the telephone, and Mrs Fellowes and I took our chance of gossiping with happy disloyalty about the man to whom we were both so deeply attached. 'You see', she told me, 'Mrs 'ighama she very nicea, but a leetle bit dominanta, joost a leetle bit dominanta. Now Mr. 'ighama, 'e wanted to wear a cappa; but she say no, it 'ad to be a 'atta, so 'e always wore a 'atta. But now — Mr. 'ighama, 'e wear a cappa.' An hour later Tommy preceded me into the hall on our way to the car in which he was going to drive me to the station, and I mused on how little he knew of what I knew as I watched him reaching up, just a thought too nonchalantly, to take the cappa down from its pegga.

I can only recall two things that happened in my second term. The first was my attempt to fulfil a duty that had suggested itself to me in the course of the Christmas vac; I had been somewhat disquieted by certain rumours I had heard about a friend called Terence Rattigan, and I thought I should at least try to talk him into considering a more orthodox way of proceeding. So at an early point of the term I went round to see him, fully expecting to make a mess of my errand but determined to get it behind me. I was even worse at the job than I had feared, and after several minutes of watching my squirmings and wrigglings on his armchair and listening to a speech that started again and again but never got beyond its prefatory 'Er, er', Terence compassionately took charge. 'Out with it, Mike! What *is* it you're trying to say?' So out it all stumbled, and Terence was very courteous about it, and then we talked about other things. No blood had been spilt and honour had been almost satisfied.

The other event was the Women's Oxford and Cambridge Lacrosse Match, for it took place in Oxford that year, and Ruth was in the Cambridge team. I naturally did a bit of boasting about her, and I made it clear to my companions that they were expected to go and see her play. But it didn't all go as I intended, for when the day came I was in bed with flu; the companions loyally trooped along and watched, but there was no one to tell them that the names and positions were wrongly given on the card, so that they came away highly amused by my simple ideas of what constituted an attractive sister.

With the summer term the problem of exercise arose again, in a form which I was glad not to have foreseen; for there were no fewer than twelve Authentics in the college that year, and there were only two cricket elevens. The sun was shining, the trees of the front quad were in blossom, Trinity and Oxford had never been more desirable; and I was to have no cricket. The truth was so unacceptable that I had to do something to change it, and I took one of the few positive actions of my indecisive life: I founded a cricket club. It was primarily based on Trinity men — me, of course, Pat Macrory, Dick Dagnall, my stair-fellows Kit and Aubrey Aitken, Terence Rattigan, Bill Wynne Willson, Paul Wootton, Ian Orr-Ewing, Francis Keenlyside — but we also brought in recruits from other colleges; my own two imports were Dick Beddington and my old Leasian friend Dick Seddon, who had bowled for Sherborne. Our fixtures ranged from small village clubs to Cheltenham College lst XI, and if our own resources were inadequate for any of them we called in suitable reinforcements, always on the tacit understanding that the contract would not necessarily be renewed. In deference to the founder and first president the club called itself The Mokes, and since donkeys are often white and like to feed in green pastures the colours were easy to choose: the cap was a brilliant emerald, with a silver moke rampant as its crest. I was allowed to be captain for the first match, but by general agreement — possibly with one dissentient voice — it never happened again.

Meanwhile I was also enjoying cricket at first remove by watching it as it was played in the Parks. There were some exceptional batsmen in that Oxford side of 1931: B. W. Hone, the captain and opener, who played in Sheffield Shield cricket in Australia; A. Melville of my own stair, later to captain South Africa and to score three successive hundreds against England, who more than any other batsman I have seen could have been said to 'flow' into his strokes; 'Tuppy' Owen-Smith, who had already played for South Africa, who you felt would have made at least a single hundred every time he went in had he not found batting so

97

easy from his first ball on that he usually became a little careless in the mid-thirties: F. G. H. Chalk, who was as classically upright and elegant as the legendary Palairet must have been, but after a bad last season at school and an indifferent Freshmen's match had only won his place in the side because Holmes and Sutcliffe had spotted him at net practice. There was also a rather tragic figure called Denis Russell, who wore a Middlesex cap and year after year was tipped as a 'dead cert'; but he found the weight of public expectation too much for him, and the necessary runs never came. In a desperate attempt to retain him Hone tried to make more of his left-arm bowling, then frustrated his own good intentions by keeping him on too long against Frank Woolley on the hunt. The way back from the Parks goes past Rhodes House[1], and as I was leaving one day there was a great shiny black car standing outside it. I looked in casually at the window, and then I looked hard; for the man I was looking at was Albert Einstein, and I gaped at that magnificent head till the Senior Proctor had to wave me away.

Towards the end of that term my mother made her one appearance at Oxford, accompanied by two of her sisters. She did nothing to disgrace me this time, unless Philip Landon was by an open window when I was showing her the bust of Cardinal Newman in the garden; for the sight of that noble face brought out all the staunch Protestant of her inheritance, and in her brief address to its owner she used a word which he couldn't often have heard from his fellow-theologians. At one point when I was not about, my aunts asked my mother why it was that nobody ever dropped in to see me; could it be that dear Michael had no friends? The reason was obvious of course: the friends knew what was going on and were keeping well away. Once I had learnt of my aunts' inferences I gave the friends new orders, and if my door thereafter wasn't sought with quite the frequency of messengers bringing tidings to Job, the bursting in with an apologetic 'Oh, I'm sorry, Mike, I didn't know' happened just often enough to silence the amital tongues and appease my mother's pride.

1. I have never quite understood how Cecil Rhodes came to be admitted to Oxford at all, for according to a trustworthy academic source he could make nothing of the statutory Greek translation paper. He did find one two-word fragment in the middle of the paper which he thought he could attempt, but even that was beyond him; instead of translating ''Ρωραῖοι δέ' as 'but (or 'and') the Romans' he could only offer 'the Pomaeans indeed'.

This story gives an ironic twist to the extraordinary way in which, up to my day at least, the authorities at Rhodes House gave warning to any visiting stranger that he was not supposed to smoke on the premises. Instead of displaying a simple English notice to that effect where anyone might look for it, they expected the stranger to interpret a Greek inscription on the floor of the central hall — a task made harder by the fact that the operative compound is not to be found in any lexicon. It is hard to believe that the great statesman himself would have put his pipe out at the sight of that inscription.

The first half of that Long Vac belongs to my father, for it brought the fulfilment of his two most cherished ambitions.

In the first place he scored the one and only century of his life. In filial piety I must add that while still up at New College he had run out of partners at 98, and that when he was in his late forties I had myself seen him declare before he knew that he was on 94 — a mistake that he would not have made if he had been satisfied to get his runs at a sober countable rate like his son. But those who know the experience all say that there is something about that third figure which lifts it into a different category from all your pedestrian 99s, and though my father had had to wait some thirty eight years for it I am pretty sure that he would have regarded those thirty eight years as years well waited.

But it was the County Court judgeship that was really important. For some little time he had been given to understand that a letter from the Lord Chancellor would be shortly on its way, and the family had been living in constant expectation of the call from his Manchester chambers that would tell us the good news. I was in when it eventually came, and I can still hear the charwoman's excited cry: 'That's 'im! I know 'is ring!' We were all of course affected by the promotion, but it meant far more to him than it could possibly have meant to the rest of us: he had won a new standing, he had shown the world that he was something better than a struggling barrister after all, and though he was never going to be a rich man he had at least the security of a fixed salary, and would no longer be dependent on those irregular payments which his clerk was so slow at collecting and which were so pitifully inadequate when they came.

His circuit was Derbyshire, and for the best part of five years he spent the week living in lodgings in Derby and only rejoined his family for the week-ends; he travelled third-class, but he was always careful to be seen emerging from a first-class door when his registrar met him at Derby Central. In the end he found the house he was looking for in Darley Dale, near Matlock, and by the middle of 1935 he, my mother, Penelope and myself were happily installed in it. On his first return to Bowdon he ran into an old friend whose speech was broad Lancashire but whose favourite book was Debrett, and their opening exchange ran thus:

' 'as the Duchess of Devonshire called yet, 'arold?'
'No, Freddy.'
'Mm. 'as the Duchess of Rutland called?'
'No, Freddy.'
'Mm. 'as Lady Belper called?'

'No, Freddy.'

'Mmm. *(Lunga pausa.)* Thought they wouldn't.'

My own vac went smoothly enough for a time. I was keeping tolerably close to Tommy's prescription of five hours' reading, and when I wasn't working, or taking the constitutional he also prescribed, I could usually be found either at the cricket club or at the Mathias's. J. Lloyd Mathias was the best of all my father's many good friends, a great and rich character if ever there was one, who as a former rugby international answered my still not outgrown need of having a hero to worship; and his wife Dolly and his daughters Beryl and Squib never failed to make me welcome. I didn't feel that I was exploiting their good nature because I could always repay their hospitality by playing the piano. I loved them all, and I was never happier than when I was at their house.

But before that vac was half-way through I knew that I was in for trouble, and trouble far more serious than anything I had had before. On my return to Oxford I did my best to conceal my condition, but it was soon plain that all was not well with me. The college inevitably came to hear of it. Tommy removed my name from the list of his candidates for the Craven and Ireland, and in early December I was given the choice between staying up for the fortnight of term remaining and going straight home; whichever I did I should need a medical certificate before I could be allowed back. In the event I stayed; Pat Macrory's version of the story is that it took me two weeks to pack, but my own memory is that I just couldn't make up my mind.

The trouble remained with me for nearly all the Christmas vac: though it was seldom bad enough to prevent me from working it was always there — while two thirds of my mind were with the *Medea* the other was with the thoughts I didn't like thinking. But somehow or other the pressure eased as the days went on, and I was given that certificate. I returned to a more or less normal Oxford existence, and in a way I enjoyed it with a keener relish because I was still aware of the shadows in the background, rather as the reader of *Oliver Twist* savours the cosiness of Mr Brownlow's fireside the more for knowing that a dark shape has just passed the window.

In March I got my first, with only one beta in the last paper to flaw my record in the compositions and unseens, and B + ? + as my lowest mark in the prepared work. But it had been a close thing, and for the rest of my undergraduate days neurosis of some kind and degree was rarely far off; I was never to know again the glad confident morning of my first year.

That February I had been approached by Edward Bischoff with a proposal. His mother had written to say that she was intending to take him on a cruise in the Mediterranean and would be delighted if one of his friends could come as well; he had written back to say that none of his friends could afford to do so; she had written back in her turn protesting that surely one of them could afford to come as her guest: in short, Eddie asked me, would I be the requested volunteer? For once I found a decision easy to make.

A little more than a fortnight after Mods I was in the Bay of Biscay. The sun was shining from a blue sky, and the Bay was by its own standards peaceful; but it had developed a steady long roll — long enough for you to wonder as you lay in your bunk whether it was ever going to reverse itself — and most of the passengers kept their cabins that day. It was because I was still on my feet that I was chosen to be a member of the Sports Committee; the chairman was a middle-aged Lancashire business man, who would answer my self-important 'When do we meet?' with 'We met at ten this mornin'. But the work of that committee was to lead to what was admittedly one of the obscurer records in the history of British athletics, but for sheer inexplicability can rarely have been equalled: I won the Potato Race, and my earnest opponent in the final was a Midlands sprints champion. Zeno was vindicated: the tortoise did outrun Achilles.

I said earlier that in some ways my own mother had been the last sort of mother a boy would choose to have, but Edward could never have had the same complaint about Mrs Bischoff: one to whom the doing of right things came so naturally would have found it hard to do a wrong one. She was firm underneath, you knew that, but firm in a way that could never have hardened her essential kindness; it tempered your affection with respect, but went no further that that. Her gentle brown eyes were also perfect; there would have been something amiss if so gracious a person had not been beautiful as well. Once I had learnt not to be too hearty too early in the morning Edward and I were never out of accord, and if the little pleasantries we shared were sometimes less mature than we supposed there was one innocent moment that I like to think we might still enjoy; at dinner one night I asked our waiter to send me 'the wine chap', and it gave us great pleasure the next morning to see that the first course at breakfast was announced on the menu as 'Bath Chaps'.

The roof and crown of that voyage was unquestionably Tangier. I had already seen Florence, I was later to see Rome and Venice and Urbino, and if you take into account all the varied treasures that those great cities have to offer then of course they out-top the

101

comparison; but for pure immediacy of impact, with the gentle ascent through terraced orange groves to the shining white buildings of the town above — not to mention the luxuriant hinterland to be traversed after lunch on donkey-back — I have never known anything to equal the Tangier of 1932. In contrast the Casablanca of the day before had had all the lively excitement of a new and rich experience but no suggestion of beauty, and Algiers, which followed, looked just sordid. But Majorca came near to rivalling it, for Palma was at that time unspoilt, and the long carriage-ride to Chopin's villa gave the suggestion that the island was all trees; it might even have dislodged Tangier in my esteem if the day had not been rainy throughout. That rain continued for what little remained of the cruise; but it hardly mattered, for the best was now behind. In Gibraltar, what with the weather and the speech of the inhabitants, only the sight of that glistening great rock forbade the illusion that we were already back in England, and the dilapidated splendours of the Lisbon royal palace served only to depress — the tarnished gilt and red of the décor suggested the taste of a megalomanic Edwardian landlady.

Edward came to spend a few days with me in Bowdon afterwards, and he was still there when the result of Mods appeared in the papers. As he and I were discussing the news in an Altrincham café that morning a loud voice broke in from an adjoining table (it came incidentally from the mother of the boy who had made the remark about Ruth and her party manners): 'What has Michael Longson done now?' It was gratifying indeed to be thus advertised in front of my friend; but I was never to hear anything like it again.

I have little excuse to offer for what followed. True, I had heard from somebody at some time that all a sixth-form master needed was a first in Mods; but the briefest reflection would have told me that an at least respectable sequel would also be required, and that the most linguistically inclined sixth-form master could well be expected to teach ancient history. As it was I postponed that reflection as long as I could. In the summer term after Mods I viewed Greats much as a very young child views old age, a thing which would have to be faced in its own good time but need not be considered yet. My line was that of Frank Sidgwick's 'On the Cabin Roof':

> Sometime in the days gone by
> I did something; was it I?
> Do not ask: I have forgot
> Whether it was I or not.

Sometime I shall have to do
Something else, but so will you.
Do not argue, but admit
That we need not think of it.

Meantime, while my contemporaries were applying themselves responsibly to their new work, I was taking belated breakfasts at the Cadena, contentedly munching my grape nuts and poring over Cardus's latest report in the *Manchester Guardian*. On the third Monday of the term I did make an attempt to start a habit of going to lectures; but the chapel clock struck ten even as I passed beneath it. I said to myself 'Ah! The gods have spoken', and the attempt was not repeated for the rest of the term.

Once I got down to the philosophy I found myself deeply interested in it, in thinking and talking about it, that is: I was only to find out when it was too late that I never gave the officially or unofficially prescribed reading the intensive study it demanded. Though we were supposed to think for ourselves our licence to do so was in one way curiously restricted; we were expected never to stray too far from the sceptical principles of idealism, which forbade us to accept the evidence of our senses without question, like the 'plain man' to whom we were by definition superior; but we didn't necessarily have to follow Bishop Berkeley in believing that nothing existed independently of the mind — and even he had run into trouble when he tried to identify that mind, as the two limericks about the tree in the quad illustrate. The logical conclusion of such idealism was of course solipsism, for no man has any certain proof that other people exist, but I never had the pleasure of meeting a convinced solipsist; it would have been interesting to see how he could conduct a conversation with what he believed to be merely something he had thought up for himself. My own creed was based on as much as I could understand of the phenomenalism of Kant: there *was* a universe independent of man, but since his understanding of it was qualified by the limitations of his own mind no one could ever know what it was really like. I might be able to accept that still did it not threaten the validity of most aesthetic judgements; if any philosophy is going to insist that a symphony or a picture may in fact be something very different from what I am hearing or seeing, then hang up that philosophy.

There was a touch of arrogance about the Oxford philosophy of that time, and I don't see that our own dear tutor, Henry Price, can be exonerated. He had all the human virtues that I know of, and in all other ways he was as humble as anyone could have asked; even his tutorials were on the surface mainly social affairs, with himself acting as *primus inter pares,* more the guide than the instructor; but every now and then you were aware of a little hard edge of intellectual self-certainty thrusting up from beneath. When I lunched with him in New College shortly before the war he surprised me by saying of T. H. Green and his set: 'You know, I sometimes think that those old Oxford idealists had a certain broad wisdom which we haven't got.' But even then he had to revert to his old self by adding with his familiar chuckle, 'The trouble is that they always had such odd *reasons* for believing what they did.'

As a bachelor don he loved entertaining, and he did it very well: always affable and benign, always likely to come out with some remark that no one else in the world would have thought of. You learnt on those occasions that every detail in his life was the result of some acute mental process; the long paper spills in the jug on his mantelpiece had been constructed on the nicest calculations, and if he didn't always use one of them to light the pipe in his mouth it was because empirical research had shown him that when he felt he had had enough tobacco a little paper stuffed into the bowl could make an agreeable substitute. He was a very moderate drinker, for he had a theory that alcohol usually intensified whatever frame of mine one was in at the moment, and his own frame of mind was usually 'rather *evil'*. He was always the philosopher, even on the golf-course or the road; the golf-course would be the Frilford Heath nine-holer, and the road would be the road to it. If his drive from the tee trickled a mere fifteen yards at an angle of forty five degrees he would reduce the incident to its proper place in the scheme of things by remarking, 'Dear me! how very odd!'; and once, when his 'I always feel rather frightened at this corner' was promptly followed by the appearance from nowhere of a fast car which missed us by inches, all he added was, 'Dear me! with reason this time.'

One Saturday afternoon the road was not to Frilford but to a point in the Oxfordshire countryside from which he and I could take a walk. Before starting on it we turned in for coffee at a little wayside shack, and Henry was fascinated by a technicology that was new to him: 'Oh, so you pour it out of a *bottle.* That's *very* interesting!' As we were passing a wood we found that the steep track through it was being used for a motor-cyclists' hill-climb; there were many loud machines and many vocal spectators, and it was obvious that the event was being taken very seriously indeed by all concerned. 'Dear me! said Henry. 'What anti-social behaviour!'. When we rounded the edge of the wood we came in sight of a river from which a whole wedge of swans was taking off in ordered succession, and once again Henry's response was philosophically perfect. He was speechless.

Towards the end of the thirties he was elected to the Wykeham chair of Logic. He had his misgivings about accepting the post; as he explained in his reply to my letter of congratulation a professor was 'expected to set a lead', and he doubted his ability to do so. His doubts were in some degree justified by the event, for the philosophy prevalent in post-war Oxford was a philosophy very different from his. I last saw him about 1950, and my impression was of a saddened and prematurely old man; the meeting-place he had for some reason chosen was a bench under Headington Hill, and the raindrops fell cheerlessly round us from the autumnal trees as each of us sought in vain for something undepressing to say. [1]

I have never quite understood why I was so obstinately determined to be bored by the history. True, the accounts of it given in the Cambridge Ancient History were too often interrupted by scholarly qualifications or digressions to give one what is known as 'a good read'; but there was nothing intrinsically dull about the academic problems themselves, and if what I wanted was a compelling straightforward narrative, what greater exemplars of the craft were there than Herodotus and Tacitus and Thucydides of the sixth and seventh books?

Our history tutor, Ronald Syme, was after his own fashion as good company as Henry Price, but apart from tutorials we saw much less of him; presumably he was more self-sufficient, and didn't share Henry's need of undergraduate society. He was never less than friendly, but it is perhaps significant that though he didn't overtly object to our familiar use of his Christian name he was the only one of our three tutors not to respond in kind. We enjoyed his wit and admired his obvious brilliance, and if we failed to foresee in him the monumental figure he has since become the fault was not wholly ours; for the role he played in those days was that of the slightly frivolous, even slightly cynical young don who regarded nothing outside his own discipline as of any great consequence. He was without doubt an exceptionally good teacher, and very possibly a great one; but that was one of the things I never allowed myself to learn.

After our second summer term Pat and I moved out to a house in the Banbury Road which stood a few yards to the north of the

1. I retain the above because it faithfully describes my last experience of a well loved friend, but I have since been given reason to think that I was wrong over the implied inference: in a recent talk with Lord Quinton I learnt that Henry was to hold his chair for another ten years yet, and that he never lost his vitality or the devotion of a stout band of followers. Perhaps Henry and I were both having an off-day, like the weather; he may even have thought *me* a saddened and prematurely old man.

Keble Road corner and faced a dangerous establishment known as the Old Parsonage, where only Trinity men lived and if any work was done it had to be done by stealth. Pat brought with him a fellow Cheltonian called Leslie McGregor, an intelligent, sturdily built and square-faced young man who looked far older than his nineteen years and thought himself far older still. Leslie and I had little in common apart from our both being friends of Pat Macrory's and both being amicably inclined, but we got on together well enough. One day when I mentioned that I was not so strong a man as my father he shook his head sagely and commented, 'Ah! Degenerating stock.' Yet even that I took without protest: I couldn't be bothered to point out that the human animal was usually assessed on rather less simple lines than cattle or drayhorses. The floor above ours was tenanted by Geoff Simmons and Bim Thornton, two quietly humorous and congenial men from Oriel who dropped in on us every now and then and were never unwelcome. The gramophone still played its part, though the tunes had changed; those we put on now were 'We've Got the Moon and Sixpence' (the H.M.V. version was the more brilliant, the Columbia one the truer to melody and feeling), 'Good Night, Sweetheart' and 'Love is the Sweetest Thing', though we also found time for the lubricious yodellings of Douglas Byng and an unusual American record on which the frustrated suitor announced the threat: "Gonna lay your head on a railroad line, Let the train come along and pacify your min'." I had my own private broodings — as the year went on I became vaguely aware that I wasn't working hard enough, yet I seemed incapable of achieving the required 'accelerando' — but I never allowed such thoughts to spoil my enjoyment of the company. Those were good days.

By the end of that October Leslie was in trouble. There had been an earlier incident connected with his car, and he had been forbidden to drive it again until further notice; but he cheerfully ignored the ban, and he was seen. When faced with the charge by the Proctors he exclaimed, 'What? Has my twin brother been driving in Oxford *again?*' and the defence was accepted in tribute to its sheer audacity. A week or two later he spent a night in town after extorting from our landlady a promise that she would report him as having been present in his lodgings; but this time he was less fortunate, for once the pressure of his dominant will was removed her conscience reasserted itself, and she did what she now saw to be her duty. Shortly afterwards I had occasion to see the President myself: at the beginning of every Michaelmas term there was an internal exam (known as 'collections') on the work we were supposed to have done in the Long Vac, and Syme had spoken critically of my performance at the subsequent college meeting. Blinks delivered the due reprimand, and then came to what was much more on his mind: he was deeply worried about McGregor L. All the precedents demanded that he should take a stern line, but he knew that Leslie was a fundamentally solid person, and in his case there was a special consideration: 'You see, he *is* such a baby!' explained Blinks. It was as ironic as it was amazing: here were the President, whose difficulties of communication had won him the repute of being less than human, and the undergraduate, whose belief in his own maturity had persuaded almost everybody else to share it; yet the old man turned out wiser than any of us, and it was his human perceptiveness that enabled him to see through the man-of-the-world exterior to the boy within, and so eventually to make the right charitable decision. I doubt if Blinks would have cared much for Coventry Patmore's 'I will be sorry for their childishness,' but such was the principle he acted on.

In the early new year we had an unexpected visit. Alan Gilg and his friend Walter Kay, a Rhodesian air pilot, were on their journey by Morris Minor from Liverpool to Cape Town — through deserts, warrior tribes, everything — and Oxford was on their route. Their achievement was enthusiastically acclaimed in South Africa, and both at Johannesburg and Cape Town they were met by great fleets of commercial cars which escorted them into the cities. Some years ago Yorkshire TV's enterprising producer, Barry Cockcroft, used their story in his series *Once in a Lifetime:* you saw a replica of that Morris Minor coming in at the drive of Alan's house near Hereford, then you watched the two elderly heroes reliving their old experiences as they were shown the film that he had taken at the time. You wouldn't have known that Alan was already mortally ill (he never saw the programme), though you might have noticed that the wrong man had been at the wheel of the car. Cockcroft was also highly interested in the diary which Alan's son Andrew found hidden away somewhere: he saw that with a little editing its lively and graphic pages would make a very readable book, which he got published in the R.A.C.'s Overseas Travel Books series under the title *Turn Left — the Riffs have Risen.*

But there was one point which Cockcroft can't have known about, for it was mentioned neither in his programme nor in his epilogue to the book. Alan used all his remaining capital to finance the venture, but he intended to do more than recoup his expenses by selling the car back to Morris's; it was going to stand in a showroom window with its feat of endurance and his own name emblazoned on it in bold white paint, and they were going to reward him handsomely for the advertisement; indeed the firm's representatives in both those major South African cities gave him lavish assurances to that effect. But neither he nor they had taken the precaution of sounding Head Office on the point, and when Alan wrote to Miles Thomas on his return to England he received the curt answer: 'Dear Mr Gilg, I cannot see why you think I should be interested in the purchase of a second-hand car.'

Pat and I played a good deal of golf that summer, either against each other or with Henry Price, and I was also finding cricket far easier to come by than it had been two years before; I even scored a few runs from time to time, though the late Bishop of Lynne told me that a fifty for the scholars against the scouts didn't count. But as the term went on the overriding concern was how Leslie was going to fare in his Law schools: would he get that fourth, or would they plough him? During the ordeal itself interim reports passed continually between Pat and me: 'Seen Leslie?' 'Yes, Plough's down the drain.' 'Seen Leslie?' 'Yes. Plough's on again'. I rather fancy he got a third — and there were still honourable fourths going then.

A fortnight before the vac Pat sold me his Morris Minor two-seater for £5. It was for summer use only since it had no lights; within two months I had to spend a further £4 on getting the brakes relined; he did me, he knew he was doing me, and he admits it. But that purchase was to save my life.

In the following summer, driving somewhere in the depths of Oxfordshire, I surmounted a small ridge to find the narrow country lane ahead of me blocked by a vast hay-wain, much too close for my still fallible brakes, and I solved the problem by bumping my mudguards from bank to bank until I came to rest two feet behind the wain. Eight years later I was in far graver peril: I was now riding an army motor-cycle down the longest and steepest hill I had ever seen, and my machine was utterly out of control, for I was in neutral, and I hadn't learnt how to use the brakes. But once again there was a grass bank, and I had just enough presence of mind left to remember my earlier ingenuity. I miscalculated the angle, so that I hit the bank not with the front wheel but with the inside of my left foot, and when the instructor who had come back to look for me lifted the bicycle off my leg the foot was pointing uphill instead of downhill, and the boot was red instead of black. My walking has been somewhat unconventional ever since, but even to limp you have to be alive.

I never knew till many years afterwards what trouble it had given Pat to find our fourth year digs: '*I* had to do it all, of course,' he told his wife; 'Mike could never have done it for himself.' I suppose the Oxford landladies, used to copious supplies of third year men, liked to accept their lodgers in clumps, and two stray fourth year men were not held to be a quorum. All I had gathered at the end of the previous term was that digs had been found in the Abingdon road; and since I didn't even know where the Abingdon road was I didn't realise the implications of Number 174. But my goodness, those digs were a long way from the centre of Oxford. There was a bus of sorts, but it obeyed strange rules of its own; my memory is of many weary walks back from dinner in Hall down that long, long trail. One night, when returning rather later than usual, I had an experience that complemented my brief acquaintance with Einstein. There was a poster outside the Town Hall announcing that Stravinsky was conducting some work of his own there that night; the concert was just over when I rounded the corner at Carfax, and Stravinsky was coming out by the side entrance. I had to wait on the kerb while the composer was escorted along a stone pathway some four inches lower to the car awaiting him, and as I gazed down at him I mentally addressed him as 'You little *rat!*' I recalled that silent apostrophe with some pleasure when I learnt that he regarded it as near blasphemy if anyone outside his family called him Igor.

To me, if not to Pat as well, all that last year was oppressed by a sense of Götterdämmerung, though the friend who made that crack about the invisible moustache might have challenged me to name the gods. It was the custom of men living out of College to lunch from time to time in the rooms of second year friends, but now the young people who were lording it in Trinity were the freshmen of the year before; Pat and I hardly came as ghosts to trouble joy, but we did feel that our sons were inheriting us. In our digs we could never forget the imminence of Greats; Pat had no thought of the first in ancient history which his later achievements show he might have won, but he was determined to secure a good second, while I, after another college meeting and another visit to the President, was now making serious attempts to ward off a third. In our hours of ease we could usually enjoy the company of the three Queen's men above us — Colin Dilwyn, brilliant and witty, though he often seemed slightly discontented by some cause or causes unknown; Arthur Burrell, imperturbably tolerant and benign; Bill Koren, a wise and urbane American southerner with a purse that enabled him to play us *'O bella figlia del amore'* on a single-sided 10" H.M.V. white label record — but nothing could quite dispel the knowledge that our days at Oxford were nearing their end and the twilight was steadily deepening.

We noticed in October that a course of lectures was to be given at 5.15 once a week by the Lincoln philosopher, Harold Cox, and since we had often lunched or dined at Harold's liberal table we thought we ought to give him a try. But he had barely been speaking for five minutes before we understood only too well why the lectures were given at that unfashionable hour and why there were only five disciples present beside ourselves, and we agreed afterwards that not even the duty of friendship could demand our further attendance. How many of the faithful were there at the second lecture, or at what rate the returns continued to diminish, we were in consequence never able to know; it may well be that the course ceased altogether as abruptly as that given by a certain German Professor of Sanskrit, who on being asked by his Principal why he had stopped lecturing so early in the university year answered very reasonably, *'Sanskrit dauert nicht langer.'* But if we treated Harold Cox badly we treated the kindly Mrs King even worse. The trouble was her scrambled eggs, designated *en masse* by Pat as 'the chalk pit'; we resented their perpetual reappearance more and more as the days went on, and in the end I fell in with Pat's suggestion that we should find a bus which would take us to the corner of the Broad in time for breakfast in Hall. I don't think we realised quite how cruel we were being to poor Mrs King till she surprised us by saying, without any rancour, 'Mr. Macrory, why didn't you *tell* me you didn't like my scrambled eggs?' Breakfast was in any case the only meal we ever ate at 174, for there was no point in travelling so far for lunch, and most third and fourth year men usually dined in college. I took care however to avoid turning up for dinner in time to say grace; I was still not sure that I had wholly outgrown my schoolboy weakness of giggling, and for the Senior Scholar to disgrace himself thus when exchanging Latinities with his President in front of a full and silent Hall — no, I didn't dare risk it.

In the Christmas vac I began my quest for future employment; it should have been over in about a month, but in the event it took almost seven. I had no hesitation over what school I wanted most: it was Eton, where a number of scholars with more than I had to offer were perfectly contented with a few top divisions and a sprinkling of Collegers among their private pupils. Failing Eton, my ambitions were a little uncertain; I should have liked a good sixth form-mastership, but I was prepared to accept anything that might eventually lead to one.

It was always understood in College that if you wanted to get back to Eton you had to win Marsden's support, so his testimonial was one of the first I applied for. In his reply he wrote, 'I didn't know you were going in for teaching. What sort of work have you in mind?' My father was much excited: 'Marsden once told me that as a Newcastle Scholar you could have a job at Eton whenever you wanted. You write the right letter back, and you'll be there in September'. Alas, the right letter I may have written, but I put it in the wrong envelope. As Marsden read that abjectly apologetic missive beginning 'Dear Mrs. Pearson' he must have concluded that I was still as I had ever been, for I heard no more of the matter.

(Some years afterwards, when I felt that I had more or less proved myself, I approached H.K. again, and I now found him co-operative; he even wrote 'Your faults were mainly just youthfulness,' which was more charitable than true. Shortly after his letter came another from Alington's successor Claude Elliot, who told me that he had no classical vacancies at the moment, but when he had he would ask me to come and see him. But then the war intervened, and by the time it was over I had for a technical reason become too old. If Eton was still anything like the Eton of my youth, when the line between masters and boys was strictly drawn, I was probably the wrong man for it anyway; the kind of discipline I liked was an essentially sociable kind, which worked well and even happily with the right people, but even in a modified form could not safely be applied to lesser breeds without the law.)

I was in the course of applying to another school towards the end of the Easter vac when Ruth drew my attention to my testimonial from Higham. I had been deeply disappointed by that testimonial myself already. It was far and away the most important of my five, and I had expected an authoritative, detailed and favourable assessment of my merits as a pure classic — indeed had I known what Tommy was going to say to my father in June I should have been justified in expecting quite a bit more than that. Instead the document so far as I remember it ran as follows:

> 'Despite a short period of ill-health (now a thing of the past) his sound Eton training and a natural gift for composition enabled him to win a first in Classical Honour Moderations in March 1932.
> 'A reaction which set in after these concentrated efforts has hitherto impeded his work for Greats. On the personal side I have always found him very agreeable ... I think it possible that he might be a really stimulating sixth form master.'

For a man who was to become the best Public Orator within memory this was a very strange exercise in communication. Why had he thought the ill-health worth mentioning if it was now a thing of the past? Why had he dismissed the main theme in the fewest words possible and damned me with praise that could hardly have been fainter? Why had he exceeded his brief by bringing in a subject that had nothing to do with his tutelage, and qualified his criticism only by a phrase suggesting that I had had to work my hardest to get a first in Mods at all? The last sentence was better, but what chance could the potential stimulator of sixth forms have after such an introduction as that?

I think I now see what the difficulty may have been. The writer of any testimonial has to be fair to two parties at once, the employer as well as the applicant; and in this case the applicant was a man whom Tommy would have been glad to recommend on purely technical grounds, but who had given anxiety to the college first by a psychological crisis of unknown seriousness and then by a prolonged period of indolence. If he said too much of the truth in one way he might be saddling a headmaster with a fatally unstable personality; if he said too much of it in the other way he might be destroying before birth a career that would otherwise have prospered. So the poor conscientious man steered his boat with the utmost caution, veering circumspectly now to this side and now to that (rather like me bumping my old mudguards against the banks of that lane), and he ended up perilously near one of the two reefs he had been so anxiously trying to avoid.

When she saw the document Ruth spoke with the authority of a professional. 'You'll never get a good job with that testimonial,' she said. 'You must get him to rewrite it without the sentence about Greats.'

I was returning to Oxford on the following Saturday; so I sent my application in with a covering note to say that four testimonials were enclosed and a fifth would be posted at the week-end. As soon as I got back to Trinity I went round to Tommy with my urgent request, and he grumbled 'I've never done this before' as he sat writing a new version in which the offending sentence was replaced by 'Of his subsequent work I leave his Greats tutor to speak'. A fortnight later I had a letter from the headmaster's secretary telling me that the job had gone to Mr. X.Y.Z. and enclosing *six* testimonials, of which *two* had been signed by T. F. Higham. I swore to myself then that Tommy would go to his grave without hearing that story, and so, dear man, he has.

That made two postal mishaps, and shortly afterwards there was (or was there not?) a third. A headmaster wrote to ask me when I could come and see him; I wrote back to say that since at that stage any day was as good as any other I could come whenever he liked; and that, as far as I knew, was the end of it. I never found my letter lurking in any nook or cranny or raincoat pocket, and surely not even I could have failed to post a letter so important as that; but the headmaster was known to be a formidable man of punctilious habits, and I didn't dare to let him know that I was awaiting an answer from him. H. H. Hardy and I would in any case never have done for each other; if he hadn't seen through me at the interview he would have done so before my first term was out, and it was probably as well that we were both spared the embarrassment of a meeting. But I had still not found a job, and the times were waxing late.

Yet even in the midst of that depressing period, with disaster looming even nearer and no means of gainful employment foreseeable beyond it, I was still to have my one night of glory. Every Trinity Monday the foundation of the college was celebrated at length by the President, the Fellows, the Honorary Fellows, one or two distinguished guests, and the scholars; there was first a short service in the chapel, then a dinner, and finally, after an hour's interval spent by the senior and junior members of the party in their respective common rooms, a symposium attended by all but the President at which speeches were made; and the principal figure throughout was the Senior Scholar. It was he who read the lesson from Ecclesiasticus, 'Let us now praise famous men and our fathers who begat us'; he who shared the grace with the President (there was no fear of giggling then, not on that night) and declaimed the noble prayer beginning *'Domine Deus, Resurrectio et Vita credentium';*[1] he who presided at the symposium and introduced the several speakers.

It was in that last phase that I came into my own and naturally enjoyed myself most. I had to wait a little before taking over as master of the ceremonies, for Tommy as Dean always began them with a short speech describing the present breed of scholars for the benefit of guests and Honorary Fellows. That year he used the similitude of flowers growing in the college garden — a quaint figure perhaps, but nobody chose to misunderstand it, and he

1. This prayer had been familiar to me for some ten years, for either in Latin or a worthy English translation I had often heard it at Eton, the only difference being that 'pro Rege Henrico Fundatore nostro' was now replaced by 'pro Thoma Pope Equite Fundatore nostro et Elizabetha consorte ejus defunctis'. My maternal grandmother had been a Pope, and on the strength of my mother's assurance I told the President that I was directly descended from the Founder. That was easily refuted by Blinks's curt 'Sir Thomas died without issue;' but I don't know that he should have disallowed even my modified claim to kinship of some kind. When I discussed the point with my distant cousin, fellow-scholar and friend Stephen Bate I found that the tradition was equally strong in his branch of the family. And even if we had both been impostors, we could have pleaded an illustrious precedent set by the poet Alexander of that name.

handled it with his habitual grace and wit: 'We have lilies from Eton; they toil not, neither do they spin.' Of my own introductory speeches there was only one that had to be prepared: Sir Arthur Quiller-Couch was on my list, and after his embarrassing maudlinism of three years before I was determined that nothing of the kind should occur again if I could prevent it. I needn't have bothered, of course. The old reprobate had also his lines prepared, and no undergraduate was going to deny him his nauseous wallow now. 'I can never come back to Trinity without going for a walk in the lime grove, and I can never do that without having to close my eyes, because there will insist on flitting in and out among the trees the shades of so many good fellows with whom I used to work and with whom I used to play.' It was worse than ever. For the rest I merely extemporised on the basis of the points that Tommy had instructed me to make, and I did it more easily than I could ever have done in later years. I was still elated throughout the long trudge back to 174, and still elated when I put head to pillow. I knew that the morning sky would disclose a world that was the old world yet, but I wasn't going to think anything like that on my night.

It was only recently that I had realised in how perilous a case I stood. I had intensified my efforts considerably since Syme had warned me in October that if I went on as I was doing I shouldn't get a second, and by May I was hoping that I might have intensified them just enough — until Syme was reported to me as saying, 'They tell me that even the virtuous Longson is becoming a little worried; and I don't want to be uncharitable, but believe me, he has his reasons.' There were two ways of getting a second in Greats; one was to take the orthodox and usual course of doing mainly beta work, with possible splashes of alpha but no taint of any gamma (and the beta work in itself demanded a higher level of intelligence and industry than the outside world ever imagined), or you could do alpha work in one subject and gamma work in the other. It was clear now that Syme did not expect me to keep free of gammas in the history, and he would have used a very different wording on both occasions if he had had reason to believe that Price held any high hopes of my philosophy; but it was on that philosophy that my fortunes would have to depend. The one chance as I saw it lay in excelling myself in the moral philosophy paper, for I had developed a theory of my own which I privately entitled agathistic utilitarianism; it was simple — I was probably far from the first to think of it — but it was also logically sound, and I was going to defend it with all the resources of ingenuity and lucid exposition at my call.

Woe was me, when the dread trial came venen the fates were

against me. All through the examination I was suffering from what was known as a heavy summer cold, the only one I ever had in my life, and the malady was at its most disabling stage on the first morning of all, the morning of the moral philosophy paper. After sixty minutes I found myself looking at five lines written at the top of an otherwise blank sheet; five minutes later I was looking at the same five lines crossed out. How I got through the paper after that I don't remember, but I can't have done the cause of agathistic utilitarianism much good. The rest went more or less predictably, not least the history; after one painful morning I suddenly stopped on my way back to college and groaned aloud, 'Did I put Solon? They *must* know I meant Cleisthenes!' Only in one of those three papers was the gamma dignified by a double plus.

When I returned to the schools for my viva a few weeks later I was greeted by three examiners only, all philosophers; the historians were eloquently absent. The spokesman said, 'The trouble with your papers, Mr. Longson, is that they were all rather short, and it wasn't quite clear how much you had actually read.' Within ten minutes it became quite clear, and they wished me good morning. Henry Price explained to me after the results were out that there had been patches of alpha in all my philosophy papers, and the philosophers had thought it might be possible to viva me up to a general alpha beta or even alpha; what could have been done with the alpha beta I didn't clearly gather, but the alpha would have certainly saved me from a third, and had their plan been as successful as that they were even going to call back the historians in the hope that they too could raise me a class, in which event I should have emerged with a first. But improbability has its limits, even in autobiography.

When my name finally appeared in the press, two classes lower than on its last appearance, I suddenly saw what I had been blinding myself to for more than two years, that my showing in Greats was no merely personal issue of my own; I had let them all down, the family that was proud of me, the college that had honoured and subsidised me, Dealtry, Alington, Lubbock, all of them. And everybody was so overwhelmingly kind about it: my mother said 'Who cares about your silly old Greats?' and sent my father in Derby a telegram reading 'Don't mind too much' which was answered by 'Who does mind?'; Henry Price wrote a magnanimous letter commiserating with me over the departure of the days when firsts in Greats were easier to come by. I knew remorse then as I had never known it before. Even in later years I have often dreamt that they have given me a chance to redeem myself by letting me go through the whole thing again, but the dream has always gone wrong; I have now more arrears than ever still to make good, and less time than ever to do it in.

In July I was offered the classical sixth-form mastership at St. John's School, Leatherhead, and a new chapter in my life was opened. It was a good chapter, but it doesn't belong to this little book.

A SELECTION FROM
POEMS WRITTEN FOR PUNCH
1933–53

The Eve of the Staff v. *School Match*
Fragment of a Common-Room Epic

Who, Simpson, who can fittingly relate
What shining honours crown the usher's state?
Ours the best seats in Hall, and ours alone
Bread one can eat and flesh no horse has known.
Within these walls none else may hope to share
The simple comforts one would find elsewhere.
Shall we not therefore vindicate our name
By seemly prowess at some manly game?
Shall we not show them that, in spite of all,
We still can kick a tolerable ball?
So shall some wondering fag be moved to say
As from the touch-line he observes our play:
'Not all inglorious on the muddied plain
The hands that wield the unrelenting cane!
These sages, steeped in *quamvis* and in *cum,*
Appear no mean performers in the scrum!
Not in quadratics only they excel,
But oh, behold them! they can hack as well!'
  Sweet Simpson, if to shun the ensanguined field
Might end our pains and lasting quiet yield,
I should not venture this unholy game
Nor yet suggest that you should do the same;
But since, alas! around the usher waits
A horrid legion of appalling fates—
Since nought may spare us the collapsive chair,
The flying dart, the butter on the stair—
Come, Simpson, come, join we the gory rout;
Between us, man, we should lay someone out!

[1935]

118

Ballade of Domestic Calamity

('Look! Our postillion has been struck by lightning' is one of the 'useful Common Phrases' appearing in a Dutch manual on the speaking of English.)[1]

To every man upon this earthly ball
   Misfortune comes, and not a soul is free;
It claims alike the master and the thrall,
   The hungry plumber and the proud J.P.,
   But never did the eye of mortal see
A tragedy more sudden or more frightening
   Than what has happened to my wife and me:
Look! our postillion has been struck by lightning!

We had attained the topmost branch of all
   In our slow progress up the social tree;
We had quite recently acquired the Hall,
   Our menial staff had swelled to twenty-three;
   And now, in this blest year of Jubilee,
When all seemed fair and every hope was brightening,
   When Lady Parks had asked us out to tea,
Our —— postillion has been struck by lightning.

1. I have never known the story of that postillion's rise to fame, so that I cannot even guess what part, if any, the preceding piece played in it. I first became acquainted with him myself in a column of the *New Statesman* in the late winter of 1934. He therefore had a highly promising start in life quite independently of anything I could do for him. But I never heard or thought of him again till June 1935, when it suddenly occurred to me that with a little manipulation in the later stanzas that useful common phrase could be made into the refrain of a ballade. The ballade appeared in *Punch* on July 5th; a week after that I received from the editor a letter about it sent to him by Rudyard Kipling, and a week after that again I received a letter from Kipling myself, in which he told me of the number of friends whom he had 'introduced to it'. It was subsequently republished (with several misprints) in the Penguin *More Comic and Curious Verse,* and I gathered some ten years ago that it was still known of at *Punch* headquarters. I have partly rewritten the last stanza to remove a technical blemish.

Not singly do terrestrial troubles fall:
    Our gardener's boy is out upon the spree;
The seventh footman thinks he is St. Paul,
    The housemaids are laid up with housemaid's knee,
    The grooms are yodelling in a nameless key,
The cook is tight, the scullery-maid is tightening,
    The under-boots has failed his Pass Degree,
And our postillion has been struck by lightning.

Envoi

    Prince, we intended for a moderate fee
To come and drown you in a pail of whitening;
    But life is life, and it was not to be,
For our postillion has been struck by lightning.

[1935]

Ballade of Chronic Insolvency

They chase me over moor and over hill,
    They follow, growling, to my very gate;
They draw my notice to 'this little bill',
    They mention 'payment at an early date';
    And through the gloom, instinct with darkling fate,
That broods beneath the moon-forsaken sky
    I see, malignant and insatiate,
The gleaming of the creditorial eye.

There are not many things that make me ill;
    My appetite is keen, my pulse sedate,
My nerves are strong, my liver sound - but still
    There is one thing I cannot tolerate;
    All Browns are subject to this curious state,
My father told me in the days gone by.
    'Your Great Aunt Maud', he added, 'used to *hate*
The gleaming of the creditorial eye'.

In vain I ransacked with burglarious skill
    The premises of Lord Augustus Tate;
In vain, with hopes of a convenient will,
    I sprinkled arsenic on my uncle's plate;
    The jemmy-merchant says he cannot wait,
The chemist presses for a prompt reply;
    I find it ever harder to placate
The gleaming of the creditorial eye.

Envoi

Prince, I will lend you 17/8,
That I may have a debtor ere I die
    On whom I too may grimly concentrate
The gleaming of the creditorial eye.

[1935]

Salopian Threnody

Again the winds of summer
　　Blow soft from Severn shore,
And out we march to battle
　　As oft in years before;
But Umpire Appleblossom
　　Turns out with us no more.

From season unto season,
　　Through many a fierce-fought day,
With ripe and kindly wisdom
　　He ruled our simple fray;
But Mumbleside protested
　　And he has gone his way.

The field stands fair as ever
　　In all its daisied pride,
But now two arms we know not
　　Proclaim a sterner wide,
And Joseph Appleblossom
　　Turns out with Mumbleside.

[1938]

Housman never wrote a *six*-line stanza in this metre, but I think he would have found it easier to forgive me than he did to forgive Vaughan Williams.

Solomon Turned Jehu

(Lines inspired by the report in February 1942 that in Dresden seventy-two judges, among others, had been conscripted as part-time tram-drivers.)

Nay, never tell me that the world is old,
    And all the glory and the dream are fled;
The years have still their wonders to unfold,
    The poetry of earth is never dead.
Though elephants decline the power of flight,
    And ancient mountains rarely skip like rams, [1]
Yet Dresden now rejoices in the sight
    Of twelve and threescore judges driving trams.

See how they argue when their cars collide,
    With many a modern instance and wise saw!
How nod their wigs as gravely they decide
    The subtler bearings of some point of law!
While the rapt Bar pursues their paths with praise
    And lauds their skill in courtly dithyrambs,
While raucous ushers clear the startled ways,
    The stern judiciary propel their trams.

Alas, I too would cross the spumy strait
    To join my lords in their careering pride;
I long to garb me in my robe of state
    And take my lovely Goering for a ride; [2]
But Dresden woos the sojourner no more,
    They love not strangers in the land of Hamm: [3]
I am a soldier and I sweep a floor;
    I may not be a judge and drive a tram.

[1942]

1. There was a wartime Disney film called *Elephants Sometimes Fly,* and the skipping mountains come in one of the Psalms.
2. 'Taking for a ride' was American gangster parlance for murdering.
3. The reference is again to a Psalm ('Jacob was a stranger in the land of Ham'), and the marshalling yards of Hamm had been very much in the news while the Germans were still preparing an invasion.

The Come-Back

For three long years they viewed my damaged limb
And 'No', they said, 'not cricket - not this year.'
I was content. I thought, 'The threads are broke
That bound my future to the tragic past;
My star at length shall dawn, and I emerge
Triumphant, to confound the scornful tongue
And garner praise from lips that wont to smile.'
And lo, the long years passed, and yesterday
They gave the verdict: 'You can try,' they said.

  Afire with zeal I sought the dressing-room;
I found the bat, I found a shirt, a glove,
A bag that might be mine, a pair of bags
That could be no one else's, and a case
Wherein reposed the Cricket Spectacles.
But then my heart misgave me, for I thought
How glass and steel may for a while withstand
Time's ageing influence, but the eye may not.
I hastened to the oracle, and cried:
'Look, seer, upon these glasses that I bear
And tell me they will stead my questing sight
Yet one brief season; for my tenuous scrip
Can scarce afford you and another pair.'
And from the shrine there came the answer back:
'Half of your prayer is granted, O my son,
And half rejected. Through the leftward disc
Your eye may match the shrewdness of the lynx,
Nor should the hawk with keener view discern
His huddling prey; the right is not so good.
Should then the bowler to the leg propel
That dire projectile, go you in, and smite
With all your mustered power; but beware,
Beware the ball that comes upon the off.'

  Avaunt, forebodings! never be it said
That I was one to faint before the fight.

The bowler may now bowl it on the off;
The umpire may not look; a thousand things
May turn the matter, oh, a thousand things.
Come pad me, glove me, to my god-like toe
Bind the grave boot, and on my forehead set
The cap's vermilion terrors; from its lair
Fetch out the score-book, and inscribe my name
In proud charactery at Number One;
And let a multitude be here convened
So great as never on the feast-day poured
O'er Nemean fields or thronged Olympia's ways,
And bid them all make thunder with their hands
And crack the vault with plaudits as I march
In regal progress wicketwards, the man
Who cannot see them on the off too well,
And all his life has missed them on the leg.

[1945]

I wanted to include this if for no other reason, in tribute to one of the best friends I ever made through cricket. Some two or three years before he won the first Victoria Cross of the war Hugh Idwal Edwards asked me, in his soft Australian brogue, what this stuff I wrote for *Punch* was like: i.e., was it any good, or was it like my ordinary conversation, 'just plain drip'? He had his answer in 1945, for within a few months of my winning my initials in *Punch* I had an unexpected letter from the Far East theatre, quoting a line from this poem (I won't say which) and adding 'It could be no one else'. He was a very great person, and when I read his obituary in August 1982 I mourned him as I have mourned few: I had had no hopes of ever seeing him again for over forty years, but at least he was around in the world somewhere, and now that he wasn't the world had become quite suddenly a less happy place. Any of his old Derbyshire friends would have felt the same.

Sweetness and Light

The mood is on me; pass me those reports.
Now twice three fortnights in its grim career
Has this voluminous term of ours unrolled;
The dancing nerves clang cymbals round my skull,
My liver growls; now could I write in blood.
Then up, my quill! no mute nor doubtful fame
Was ours aforetime, nor long ages back
Twelve lusty prefects in one crimson morn
The lethal point of our envenomed phrase
Hurled sheer to Hades, with what eyes they might
Soon to confront their far from ghostly sires,
A royal carnage; but my vaulting zeal
Hopes now a larger excellence, a skill
Enriched, an art more deeply perfect yet:
This time we shall not mix the papers up.
  What name is here? The minor Simpson? Nay:
A Very Fair, a Satisfactory,
A Making Steady Progress at the worst;
I seek a juicier victim. Hall of Green's:
Ah, later, when the middling holidays
Have eased my wounds, then might my honeyed lyre
Sing Hall's progressive virtues, and expound
How well he learns (and I, by inference, teach),
But not just now. Who next? Ha, Prendergast?
That toad, that newt, that doer of no work,
That silent scorner of a master's wit,
That crude and mindless heap — that Prendergast?
Tear up the other papers, this is he
My fires are stoked for. Now no weakening thought
Of tearful mother nor paternal rage
And fulminated missives to the Head
Shall daunt my purpose, nor the pictured grief
Of that grown sister (though her voice was soft,
Though soft her voice, and sweet to me her words)—
Not even that shall bend my duteous will.
In madder rout, ye nerves, your cymbals clang,

Growl on, good liver; no man ever wrote
As I shall write in this tremendous hour.
    And yet, who knows? The butterfly, they say,
Misfits the wheel, and the great bludgeon's stroke
Numbs more than pains the sense whereon it falls.
A charm more potent haply may invest
The hinted menace, and the chill reproach
Of what was left unsaid... *'A fair term's work.'*

[1945]

"It Sinks . . ."

(Written during the Great Fuel Shortage in post-war Britain)

This is the last; feed slowly then, my fire,
For where it comes from, lo, there is no more.
When this is done, you die; feed slowly then.
Now all my latent majesty of soul
Must rise to meet this crisis; let me think
Of those old sages whose exalted mind
Could soar serene above all fleshly ills,
Or him of Carthage, whom the books recount
As trained 'with equal fortitude to bear
Both heat and cold' . . . Ah, no, it steads me not;
I cannot think of those philosophers,
I do not even know the fellows' names;
And him of Carthage — who could not be such
Were only he as hot as he is cold?
Some surer shift is needed. (Out, alas!
Behold with how improvident a maw
This flame devours its last terrestrial meal!)
Let no one bid me don my wintry shorts
And grimly seek a false unnatural warmth
Through some mad 'circulation of the blood':
My blood is good blood, solidly compact
Of golden virtues, kindly, temperate, just;
But circulate — it never *circulates*.
And if it did, why goodness gracious me,
The stuff is frozen; who would like a mass
Of sullen glaciers forging round his veins?
It would bring on neuralgia, it would hurt.
And what should happen if I ran too fast
And suddenly the swelling thaw set in?
Out, horrid notion! May my foes end thus.
(Ah me, already the last fringe of black
Now reddens into fire; the end is nigh.)
I wish I were a furnaceman; I wish
I drove a train; I wish I were a thief,

A fuel thief whom no one ever caught;
I wish for twenty years before the war
I had reserved from every fire I burnt
One little lump, and stored it in a shed;
I wish I had not lit the thing so soon.
What sight is this? Ha, is my darling dead?
Ah, sweet Theridamas, say so no more!
Though she be dead, yet let me think she lives!
She should have died hereafter; she died young.
Now panic holds me; I am desperate;
I will do anything shall make me warm;
I'll set the Thames on fire, I'll burn my boats,
I'll burn my books — Ah, *Mephistopheles!*

[January, 1946]

Unwedding Presents

My festive hat, my weeds of cheerful green,
Have graced ere now full many a nuptial scene,
And many a bridegroom, many a budding wife
Have I had part in setting up for life.
From those who leave one free at will to bring
The dainty toast-rack or the napkin-ring,
To those, more shrewd, who rigidly insist
On strict adherence to some ruthless list,
Or those again at whose imperious beck
Are signed the frank commitments of the cheque,
By each and all my duty has been done.
For what return? Upon my soul, for none.

   Alas, how cruel, how unjust our lot
Whom none has bound with Hymen's envied knot!
May we not claim (though blighted, it is true)
A life for which we might be set up too?
Though no fond presence cheers our dark retreat,
No infant mirth, nor patter of small feet,
We still aspire to play at times the host,
We still use napkins, and we still eat toast.
Must we lose all Life's treasures with the best,
And, wanting one thing, therefore want the rest,
Grow bleakly old by Need and Care pursued,
And die in debt as well as solitude?

   Hear then, ye husbands, and, ye wives, attend!
Give ear, good aunts, take notice, every friend!
Four weeks from now (mark well the solemn date)
I shall confirm my bachelor's estate.
Then let your crowds be seen in Paul's high dome
(And afterwards at Fleet Street Mental Home),
And I, before your awed and pitying gaze,
To Singleness shall consecrate my days.
With all my worldly chattels I shall vow
My grateful self, none other, to endow,

And faithful yet, in poverty or wealth,
In joy, in grief, in sickness and in health,
Till night descends, and the long day is done,
To love, obey, and honour Number One.

Your answering duties hardly need be told;
But cars are useful, and I do like gold.

[1946]

Penalties

or The Anagrammatist Quits the Holy Land

Familiar country, loved this many a year,
I write thee *an epistle* ere we part;
Though with my *pen I slate* thee, yet how dear,
Image of woe, thou *leapest in* my heart!

No one could leave thee with a worse regret,
And no one *else paint* with a warmer zeal
Thy towering scenery (like an *Alpine set*)
Crowned with *neat piles* of radiant *satin-peel*.

Where the *inept seal* hunts his scaly feast,
The *silent ape* desports him in the trees,
Rapt I would roam, nor ever in the *least*
Pine by thy Jordan for my own *plain Tees*.

But now, *see pliant* bands surround my track,
Men grim to view, and more than half inclined
To take a *late snipe* at my transient back
Or push *a steel pin* deep in my behind.

So with a spirit free from all *lean spite,*
Heavy in heart I turn me to the West;
My billet here is now a *penal site,*
And I am counted but an *alien pest.*

[1947]

Goings On of an Alter Ego

Oh, when I was above myself
  I was a curious pair;
My lower feet still walked the street,
  My uppers trod on air.
Said folk 'You must come down a peg,
  We know not where you stand';
So reaching up I pulled my leg
  And took myself in hand.

Oh, when I was beside myself
  I strutted through the town
And vinous men who saw me then
  Crept home and laid them down.
But all the neighbours raised a groan
  To view my double chins;
Said folk 'We love you best alone:
  You're just a mess as twins.'

And now I march in twos no more;
  I keep myself inside,
And Jekyll rests as heretofore
  Well hidden in his Hyde.
Yet when they read this little rhyme
  I know what folk will say:
They will most surely say that I'm
  Below myself to-day.

[1949]

This was republished with a few changes in Arnold Silcock's *Verse and Worse,* and it was read on BBC 2 in 1979. I give the original version here.

Ballade of Culinary Deficiency

There gleams no gem of lustre all unblurred,
   In purest gold some tiny flaws remain;
The wise of speech are facially absurd,
   And Beauty's daughters can be just inane;
   So too with me, the Muses' favoured swain,
The pride of Thames, and Isis' darling boast — [1]
   There is one goal I never shall attain.
I have no gift for scrambled eggs on toast.

What boots the careful mixture briskly stirred,
   The measured marge and salt's adjected grain?
The secret dwells not in the printed word,
   It all depends on something in the brain.
   I put the point to housewives in the train,
I tramp to lectures and I learn by post;
   But vain the lecturer, the postman vain:
I have no gift for scrambled eggs on toast.

On certain nights high honour is conferred
   Upon my homely lodgement in Park Lane;
The voice of Wit within these walls is heard,
   And Rank and Wealth hold here their dazzling
reign.
   Then do I serve some wholesome dish yet plain,
Some artless soufflé or some easy roast?
   No: I do scrambled eggs on toast again.
I have no gift for scrambled eggs on toast.

Envoi

   Prince, why so mute? O horror! he is slain;
My lord has left me for a sterner host.
   I only trust your Highness felt no pain ...
I have no gift for scrambled eggs on toast.

[1949]

1. I now feel a little ashamed of this line, but see no satisfactory way of replacing it.

The Shropshire Misogynist

When I was one and twenty
  I heard a poet say
That sighs were his a-plenty
  Who gave his heart away;
And well his words I pondered
  And swore that, come what would,
Whatever else I squandered
  My heart was mine for good.

But never heart went better
  For keeping to oneself,
And man may shirk the fetter
  But cannot shun the shelf;
And lonely hearths lie dirty,
  And loveless roads are long,
And I am nine and thirty,
  And Housman had it wrong.

[1951]

VERSES WRITTEN FOR THE PROGRAMMES OF SHAKESPEAREAN PRODUCTIONS AT THE EDINBURGH ACADEMY

Julius Caesar, 1952

Be patient, friends! forgo the haughty sneer,
And lend our play your more indulgent ear.
Expect to-night no master of the art
To charm the vision, or to shake the heart;
No Roscius figures on the programme's page,
Nor Keen nor Wolfit treads the new-built stage.
But though we boast no mighty names like these,
Such as we are, we yet shall try to please;
Though crude the accent and though harsh the tone,
The language (mostly) will be Shakespeare's own,
And as you watch we hope that you will find
The rough effects you may have had in mind:
A Brutus stern, a Caesar amply proud,
A quiet Prompter, but a vocal Crowd.
And if some line, some cadence here and there
May break in music on the listening air;
If once or twice our action may supply
A quicker pulse, a briefly moistened eye;
If, all in all, this tale of ancient Rome
May make you glad you did not stay at home:
Then not in vain before your honoured sight
Shall this our Caesar bleed in sport to-night!

Twelfth Night, 1954

This is Illyria. Here before your eyes,
Grave auditors, a magic country lies,
   Where laughter thrives and lyric fancies throng,
   Where heads at times are weak, and passions strong,
And true love's course runs most contrariwise;

Where noble ladies mock their princes' sighs,
And maidens strut in masculine disguise,
   And major-domos grow some eight feet long:[1]
          This is Illyria.

Then who can tell, beneath these witching skies
What strange predicaments may not arise?
   Should Duke miscue, or Fool forget his song,
   Should both the Knights get all their entries wrong,
Let nothing here occasion your surprise.
          This is Illyria.

[1] The Malvolio of the production was the writer and broadcaster Gordon Honeycombe.

Hamlet, 1958

Behold, the time of our biennial play
   Returns once more as on the seasons fleet:
But now a sterner labour we essay:
   Command us not past follies to repeat.
   Farewell the routs of Windsor's busy street,
The laughing sunlight of Illyria's shore!
   From urban Scotland and the summer's heat
We take the wintry road to Elsinore.

Again, as once in Shakespeare's hallowed day,
   The armoured ghost shall stalk his royal seat;
Again the dotard minister shall pay
   The fatal forfeit of the indiscreet;
   Her watery end again the maid shall meet,
Again the pavement flow with princely gore ...
   To sombre music and the drum's slow beat
We take the wintry road to Elsinore.

We know what hazards must beset our way,
   What gins and quagmires may our footsteps greet;
We know too well how fierce will be the fray,
   The victory at best how incomplete.
   Reft now the comfort of the printed sheet,
Our wise producer may not friend us more;
   But on we must, for there is no retreat.
We take the wintry road to Elsinore.

Envoi
   Sweet gentlemen, and ladies doubly sweet,
Weep with us now, as you have laughed before!
   Share still our journey, while with hopeful feet
We take the wintry road to Elsinore!

The Merchant of Venice, 1962

Good people, do not rush away,
  Nor slip discreetly from the hall
Before the ending of our play.

'Twere only courtesy to stay
  Until the actors take their call;
Good people, do not rush away.

Your liveliest feelings we would sway,
  We hope to shake you pit and stall,
Before the ending of our play.

Our Shylock has an air, they say:
  Our Portia holds all hearts in thrall:
Good people, do not rush away,

Though many a line may go astray
  And many a luckless brick may fall
Before the ending of our play.

We have rehearsed it night and day,
  It is well written, after all.
Good people, DO not rush away
Before the ending of our play.

King Henry the Eighth, 1964

Not only those who charm the public ear
   Where Old Victoria frowns on Waterloo,
   Or Stratford flies her bravest flags anew
To greet her son in this his natal year —
Not these alone the Shade delights to hear:
   He gladly haunts the humbler stages too,
   And spends whole evenings well content to view
The rustic Brutus or the youthful Lear.

Look round: it may be in some neighbouring row
A figure sits that none would seem to know,
   And none will swear to when it first appeared;
Or in some corner of the hall there stands
A genial form that claps with soundless hands
   And smiles behind an incorporeal beard.

(Since I have never been able to accept that much of King Henry VIII was written by
Shakespeare (my own far from original views on the question of which was his last real play
should be made clear on the next page), I made the poet's quatercentenary my theme
instead.)

The Tempest, 1966

1611

Forspent with toil, and yearning to regain
The friendly quiet of his native plain,
For the last time he pauses to review,
As in a dream, the varied world he knew.
Once more he ponders with impartial mind
The baseness and the glory of mankind,
The prince, the clown, the traitor and the sage,
High-hearted youth, and garrulous old age;
And yet again he conjures to his aid
Those airy shapes of his own fancy made,
The elfin sprites of grove and hill and stream
Who flashed their radiance through that earlier Dream.

And now the tale is told; on each and all
He lets his sovereign benediction fall,
Revokes for ever the enchanter's spell,
And bids his audience and his art farewell.
His buried staff lies fathoms underground,
And deeper than did ever plummet sound
The book that wrought the miracles is drowned.

TRANSLATIONS FROM THE GREEK

The Go-Between

Fly you now, my swift mosquito,
    Fly you to Zenophilê:
Pluck her ear, and in it whisper
    This one message brought from me.

Tell her that alone and sleepless,
    Waiting through the night I lie,
While she slumbers, love unheeded:
    Rouse you, friend of poets — fly!

Tell her that, but sing it softly,
    Lest you wake her partner too,
And I learn to my discomfort
    What a jealous man can do.

Bring you but my darling hither,
    Proud the guerdon you will win:
You shall swing a club, mosquito,
    You shall sport a lion-skin.
                    Meleager (O.B.G.V. 582)

A Maltese watch-dog lies this earth below,
  Who served Eumaeus stoutly all his days.
Bull was his title while he lived, but now
  That mighty bellower treads the silent ways.
                    Tymnes (O.B.G.V. 511)

    There was a grammatical tutor
    Whose daughter encouraged a suitor.
      She proceeded to be
      The proud mother of three,
    One boy and one girl and one neuter.
                    Palladas (O.B.G.V. 634)

TRANSLATIONS INTO
LATIN AND GREEK VERSE

A Jacobite's Epitaph

To my true king I offered free from stain
Courage and faith; vain faith, and courage vain.
For him I threw lands, honours, wealth, away,
And one dear hope, that was more prized than they.
For him I languished in a foreign clime,
Gray-haired with sorrow in my manhood's prime;
Heard on Lavernia Scargill's whispering trees,
And pined by Arno for my lovelier Tees;
Beheld each night my home in fever'd sleep,
Each morning started from the dream to weep;
Till God, who saw me tried too sorely, gave
The resting-place I asked, an early grave.
O thou, whom chance leads to this nameless stone,
From that proud country which was once mine own,
By those white cliffs I never more may see,
By that dear language which I spake like thee,
Forget all feuds, and shed one English tear
O'er English dust. A broken heart lies here.

Macaulay

The Jacobite is now an ex-officer of the Pompeian Army, self-banished to Greece. The Daphnus was a river in north-west Greece, though no Roman writer seems to have mentioned it.

Quod mihi virtutis, fidei quod labe carentis,
    haec tribui iusto, nec valuere, duci.
hunc propter titulos et opes agrosque reliqui,
    et te, prae cunctis spes pretiosa bonis;
hunc propter iacui semoto litore marcens,
    dum iuveni maeror tempora cana notat;
Campanos finxi Tempe dare mota susurros
    nec iuvit memorem Daphnia ripa Padi;
nocte domus aegrum propriae ludebat imago,
    mane novo flebam somnia falsa vigil;
dum mihi corda deum nimios miserata labores,
    et requiem optatam mors properata dedit.
quisquis ad ignoti subiisti hoc forte sepulcrum,
    patria cui natum me quoque magna tulit,
te iuga per septem nunquam repetenda precamur,
    te per et his olim verba sonata labris,
pone odium: cinerem lacrima dignare vel una
    civilem. fracti busta dolore vides.

Love's Farewell

Since there's no help, come let us kiss and part.
Nay I have done, you get no more of me;
And I am glad, yea, glad with all my heart,
That thus so cleanly I myself can free.
Shake hands for ever, cancel all our vows,
And when we meet at any time again,
Be it not seen in either of our brows
That we one jot of former love retain.
Now at the last gasp of Love's latest breath,
When, his pulse failing, Passion speechless lies,
When Faith is kneeling by his bed of death,
And Innocence is closing up his eyes,
   — Now if thou would'st, when all have given him over,
   From death to life thou might'st him yet recover.

Drayton

Spes si nulla, vale post oscula dicere restat.
    nil mihi iam tecum; pars tibi nulla mei est.
pectore quin etiam toto mihi gratulor ipsi
    quod datur inlaesa rumpere vincla fide.
dispergant rapidi si quae iuravimus Austri;
    discidii pangant foedera longa manus;
si convenerimus posthac, nil lumina signent,
    neutra umquam pateat fronte superstes amor.
supremam en animam lasso trahit ore Cupido;
    lingua silet, vix iam marcida vena tremit;
iam Pudor innocuus moribundi claudit ocellos,
    ad lectosque genu deprimit alma Fides.
a, quem nunc etiam, tota lugente corona,
    si iuvet, in vitam tu revocare potes!

From 'Lord's, 1878'

(i.e. The Eton v. Harrow match.)

Feet that had sped in games of yore,
   Eyes that had guarded well,
Waited and watched the mounting score,
   And the hopes that rose and fell;
And girls put wagers and frolicking by,
   As they felt their pulses throb,
And old men cheered — but the cheering cry
   Went gurgling into a sob!

What is it — forty, thirty more?
   You in the trousers white,
What did you come to Harrow for,
   If we lose the match to-night?
If a finger's grasp, as a catch comes down,
   Goes a thousandth breadth away —
Heavens! to think there are folks in town
   Who talk of the game as play!

'Over' — batsmen steadily set:
   'Over' — maiden again:
If it takes a score of maidens yet,
   It may chance to turn the brain.
End it, finish it! Such a match
   Shortens the breath we draw.
Lose it at once, or else — A catch!
   Ah!

E. E. Bowen

The author was a famous Harrow master, who wrote a number of well-loved songs for his school, including 'Forty Years On'.

Plurimus anteactis heros spectatus in annis,
    sive arcere vigil seu celer ille sequi,
surgentem numerum patiens sine fine tuetur,
    spes dum saepe oritur pectore, saepe cadit.
deserit assuetos lusus et pignora virgo,
    plus solito vena iam trepidante sua;
clamat ovans senior, premitur sed clamor ovantis
    versaque singultum vox tremebunda ciet.
iamque quater deni, iam ter (fallorne?) supersunt.
    vae vobis, nivea veste superba cohors!
irrita polliciti nostras venistis ad aedes,
    hostis et hanc palmam si vetus ille feret.
quid si prensanti, cita dum pila decidit axe,
    fors mala praevertat quantulacumque manum?
pro caecas hominum mentes hebetataque corda!.
    sunt mihi qui ludos proelia tanta vocent?
arbiter hic 'transite' sonat, sonat arbiter ille:
    perstant clavigeri, summaque fixa manet.
bis modo si decies ultra 'transite' sonabunt,
    nescioquid capiet mens cruciata mali.
solvite nos, pueri! nimium qui talia perfert,
    hic auras anima debiliore trahit.
cedite, ni—quid fit? volat en pila—prenditur—haesit!
    liberius spirent pectora: cura, vale!

From 'Albert and the Lion'

Meanwhile Pa, 'oo 'ad seen the occurrence,
  And didn't know what to do next,
Said, 'Mother, yon lion's ate Albert!'
  And Mother said, 'Well! I am vexed!'

Then Mr. and Mrs. Ramsbotham,
  Quite rightly when all's said and done,
Complained to the animal keeper
  That the lion 'ad eaten their son.

The keeper was quite nice about it;
  'E said, 'What a nasty mis'ap!
Are you sure that it's your boy 'e's eaten?'
  Pa said, 'Am I sure? There's 'is cap.'

The manager 'ad to be sent for.
  'E came, and 'e said, 'What's to do?'
Said Father, 'Yon lion's ate Albert,
  And 'im in 'is Sunday clothes too.'

Marriott Edgar

ΠΑ. Οἴμοι, τί λεύσσω; τίς δὲ τἀντεῦθεν πόρος;
γύναι, σύ μοι' πάρηξον, ὡς λέων ὅδε
τὸν υἱὸν ἡμῶν ἀρτίως φαγὼν ἔχει.

ΜΗ. ποῖον τόδ' εἶπας; ἢ κλύουσ' ὀργίζομαι.
οὗτος σύ, θηρῶν δυσφύλαξ τούτων φύλαξ,
λέων ἐκεῖνος παῖδα νῷν ἐδήδοκεν.
ΦΥΛΑΞ.
Φεῦ.
οὐ μεμπτὸν ἐθέμην εἴ τί δυσφορεῖτ', ἐπεὶ
οὐκ εὐτυχὲς τὸ πρᾶγμα: πῶς δ' ἔγνωθ' ὅτι
ὑμῶν ὁ παῖς ἀπώλετ', οὐκ ἄλλων τινῶν;

ΠΑ. τεκμήριον χρῄζεις τι; τὴν κυνῆν ἰδέ.

ΜΗ. πρόπεμπε δεῦρο τὸν θέας ἐπιστάτην.
ἘΠΙΣΤΑΤΗΣ.
πάρειμι κληθείς, συμφορᾷ ποίᾳ δ' ἔπι;

ΠΑ. ἐδήδοχ' ἡμῶν ὅδε λέων τὸν ἔκγονον,
καὶ τοῦτο πέπλων οὐχὶ τῷ καθ' ἡμέραν
κόσμῳ περισταλέντα, τοῖς δ' ἐξαιρέτοις
σὺν οἷς ἑορτὴν θεῷ ποτ' εἰώθει ποεῖν.

155

Sonnet XC

Then hate me when thou wilt; if ever, now;
Now, while the world is bent my deeds to cross,
Join with the spite of fortune, make me bow,
And do not drop in for an after-loss:
Ah! do not, when my heart hath 'scaped this sorrow,
Come in the rearward of a conquered woe;
Give not a windy night a rainy morrow,
To linger out a purposed overthrow.
If thou wilt leave me, do not leave me last,
When other petty griefs have done their spite,
But in the onset come; so shall I taste
At first the very worst of fortune's might;
   And other strains of woe, which now seem woe,
   Compared with loss of thee will not seem so!

Shakespeare

Tunc ubi uis me sperne, sed hac nulla aptior hora,
    hac cum si quid ago sors mihi tristis obest.
deice nutantem Parcis sociata malignis,
    istaque ne posthac addita damna feram.
ne, precor, hos si quo superaro tempore casus,
    altera in enisum tu quoque bella move;
nocturno Boreae subeat ne crastinus imber,
    neu lento tritum sternere Marte para.
linquere si certum est, saltem ne me ultima linquas,
    cum mala iam poterunt haec leviora nihil:
in primis ferias; ita dis quaecumque placebunt,
    in primis dabitur pessima quaeque pati.
nunc me mille agitant, legio satis horrida, curae;
    te tamen amissa quis dolor alter erit?

On a Dead Hostess

Of this bad world the loveliest and the best
Has smiled, and said good night, and gone to rest.

Belloc

The devil was sick, the devil a saint would be.
The devil was well, the devil a saint was he!

Rabelais

King David and King Solomon
   Led merry, merry lives,
With many, many lady friends
   And many, many wives;
But when old age crept over them,
   With many, many qualms,
King Solomon wrote the Proverbs,
   And King David wrote the Psalms.

John Ball Naylor

Hoc iacet in tumulo Cornelia, nota suorum
   officiis cultrix hospitioque domus.
cui virtus tam rara fuit, cui summa venustas
   suave valedictis secubat hospitibus.

Aeger iurasti, Male, castum te esse futurum.
   heu! uigor ut rediit, tu male castus eras!

Gaudia rex Salomon percepit multa per annos;
   percepit David gaudia multa pater.
mille puellarum binis placuere favores,
   nec minor adstabat lege marita cohors.
subrepsit sed utrique parum provisa senectus.
   quid facerent, crebro cor quatiente metu?
filius ingenti scripsit Proverbia charta:
   quindecies fudit Psalmata dena pater.

Here dead lie we because we did not choose
   To live and shame the land from which we sprung.
Life, to be sure, is nothing much to lose;
   But young men think it is, and we were young.

Housman

Upon the Death of Sir Albert Morton's Wife

He first deceas'd; she for a little tried
To live without him, liked it not, and died.

Wotton

In Memoriam: April, 1915

The flowers left thick at evening in the wood
This Eastertide bring into mind the men,
Now far from home, who, with their sweethearts, should
Have gathered them, and will do never again.

Edward Thomas

Κείμεθα τῇδ᾽ ἡμεῖς τεθνηκότες, οἳ περιόντας
  τὴν πόλιν αἰσχύνειν ἀπρεπὲς ᾠόμεθα.
εἰ δ᾽ ὅδε φαῦλον ἄρ᾽ ἦν μερόπων βίος, οὐχὶ νέοισιν
  φαίνεται, οὐδ᾽ ἡμεῖς γηραλέοι θάνομεν.

Τῆσδ᾽ ὑπὸ τῆς γαίας ἱππεὺς κοιμᾶται ἀμεμφὴς
  Τέλλος Ἀθηναῖος Λυσιδίκη τε γυνή·
τὸν μὲν γὰρ πρότερον δαίμων λάβεν, ἡ δὲ θανόντος
  ζῆν ἔτ᾽ ἐπειράθη τυτθόν, ἔπειτ᾽ ἔκαμεν.

Ἄνθεα τοῦδ᾽ ἔαρος πυκινῶς φανέρ᾽ ὀψὲ δι᾽ ἀλσῶν
  ἀγκαλεῖ ἐς μνήμην ἄνδρας ἀποιχομένους·
τῆλε γὰρ εἰσ᾽ οἳ δρέψαι ἅμα σφετέραισι κόραισιν
  ὤφελον, ἕξουσιν δ᾽ οὐ πάλιν αὖτε λέγειν.

Epitaph on a Tyrant

Perfection, of a kind, was what he was after,
And the poetry he invented was easy to understand;
He knew human folly like the back of his hand,
And was greatly interested in armies and fleets;
When he laughed respectable senators burst with laughter,
And when he cried the little children died in the streets.

Auden

Poorly lived,
    and poorly died;
Poorly buried,
    and no one cried.[1]

Stranger, my wife, the loveliest lady born,
Lay sick to death. I prayed the gods to spare
My treasure, and take one whom none would mourn,
Some unconsidered slave by none held dear.
Think not the gods disdain a rich man's prayer.
That day my wife recovered. I lie here.

Quiller-Couch

[1] Epitaph in a village churchyard

Ὁιον ἔφυ τιμᾶν ὅδ᾽ ἀνὴρ τὸ τέλειον ἐθήρα,
   εὗρεν δ᾽ ἁρμονίαν εὐσύνετον πολέσιν·
ἀνθρώπων δὲ καλῶς ἠπίστατο πᾶσαν ἄνοιαν,
   παντοίας δ᾽ ἔμαθεν πυκνὰ περὶ στρατιάς:
κεἰ γελάσειε γέλως σεμνοὺς μέγας εἶχε γέροντας,
   κλαύσαντος δ᾽ ἐν ὁδοῖς νήπι᾽ ἔθνησκε τέκνα.

Πρόσθε κακῶς ἐβίωσα, κακῶς δ᾽ ἐκύρησα τελευτῆς·   .
   θαπτόμενον δὲ κακῶς οὔτις ἔλειβε δάκρυ.

Εἰς θάνατόν μοι ἔκαμνε γυνή, καλλίστη ἁπασῶν,
   ὦ ξένε, πρὸς δὲ θεοὺς τοιάδ᾽ ἐγὼ λισάμην·
"λείπετε τοὐμὸν ἄγαλμα, βροτὸν δ᾽ ἕλετ᾽ ἄλλον ἄτιμον,
   φαῦλον, ἀπένθητον, μηδέ τῳ ἀνδρὶ φίλον."
μὴ δὲ ματᾶν εὐχὰς φῇς πλουσίου, ἤματι κείνῳ
   ἡ γυνὴ ἰάθη, τῇδε δὲ κεῖμαι ἐγώ.

From 'A Midsummer Night's Dream'

Lysander.	How now, my love! Why is your cheek so pale? How chance the roses there do fade so fast?
Hermia.	Belike for want of rain, which I could well Beteem them from the tempest of my eyes.
Lys.	Ay me! For aught that I could ever read, Could ever hear by tale or history, The course of true love never did run smooth; But either it was different in blood —
Herm.	O cross! Too high to be enthralled to low!
Lys.	Or else misgraffed in respect of years —
Herm.	O spite! Too old to be engaged to young!
Lys.	Or else it stood upon the choice of friends —
Herm.	O hell! To choose love by another's eyes!
Lys.	Or, if there were a sympathy in choice, War, death, or sickness did lay siege to it, Making it momentany as a sound, Swift as a shadow, short as any dream, Brief as the lightning in the collied night, That, in a spleen, unfolds both heaven and earth, And ere a man hath power to say 'Behold!' The jaws of darkness do devour it up: So quick bright things come to confusion.
Herm.	If then true lovers have been ever crossed, It stands as an edict in destiny: Then let us teach our trial patience, Because it is a customary cross, As due to love as thoughts and dreams and sighs, Wishes and tears, poor Fancy's followers.

Shakespeare

ΛΥ. Οἴμ᾽ ὡς παρειὰν ἄρτ᾽ ελευκάνθης, κόρη.
τὰ φαίδρ᾽ ἐκεῖνα πῶς μαραίνεται ῥόδα;

᾽ΕΡ. ὄμβρου χατίζονθ᾽, ὡς ἔοικεν, ὃν πολὺν
καὐτὴ πόροιμ᾽ ἂν ὀμμάτων ῥοῶν ἄπο.

ΛΥ. αἰαῖ.
εἰ πίστ᾽ ἄρ᾽ ἦν τοι πάνθ᾽ ὅσ᾽ εἰσήκουσά πω
ἢ ᾽κ μουσοποιῶν ὅσα μαθεῖν ἐμοὶ παρῆν,
ἢ τῶν ἐρώντων αἰὲν ἦν τραχεῖ᾽ ὁδός·
οἱ μὲν γὰρ ἦσαν διάφοροι τιμῇ γονῶν,

᾽ΕΡ. φεῦ, τοὺς ἀμείνους συζυγεῖν τοῖς χείροσιν.

ΛΥ. τοὺς δ᾽ οὐ ξυνῆψεν ἡλίκων ψυχῶν χάρις,

ΕΡ. πικρὸν τόδ᾽, ἢν ξυνῶσι γηραίοις νέοι.

ΛΥ. τοῖς δ᾽ αὖτ᾽ ἐνίκων αἱ φίλων δυσβουλίαι·

῾ΕΡ. λυπρὸν δὲ καὶ τοῦθ᾽, ὃς κατ᾽ εντολάς γ᾽ ἐρᾷ.

ΛΥ. αἰθαίρετος δ᾽ εἰ ᾽κυρσε σύμφωνός τ᾽ ἔρως.
μάχη νιν ελόχησ᾽ ἢ νοσήματ᾽ ἢ μόρος,
ὥστ᾽ ἢν ὀνείρου ξυντομώτερος μονῆς,
ψόφου βραχίων, ὠκὺς ὡσπερεὶ σκιά,
οὐδ᾽ ἀστραπῆς θᾶσσόν ποτ᾽ εὐφεγγὲς σέλας
ὀρφνὴν διῇξεν, ἥπερ ὡς ὁρμῇ μιᾷ
πᾶσαν προφαίνει γαῖαν οὐρανόν θ᾽ ὁμοῦ,
εὐθὺς δέ, καὶ πρὶν τῷ πέλας δεῖξαί τινα,
σκότου γνάθοισι φροῦδός ἐσθ᾽ ἡρπασμένη·
οὕτως τὰ λαμπρὰ διὰ τάχους ἀπόλλυται.

῾ΕΡ. εἰ κοινὰ τῶς ἐρῶσι τοῖ᾽ ἄρ᾽ ἦν παθεῖν,
ἀρηρὸς εἶπας τοῦτο κἄφυκτον λάχος·
σφαλεῖσιν οὖν ἀνεκτέ᾽, ὡς πειρωμένοις
ἔρωτος οἰκεῖ᾽, ἐξ ἴσου τ᾽ εἰωθότα
ὡς καὶ στεναγμούς, δάκρυα, φροντίδας, λιτάς,
χὦσ᾽ ἄλλ᾽ ὁμαρτεῖν δυσμόρῳ φιλεῖ πόθῳ.

From 'Othello'

Gratiano.   What is the matter?
Othello.   Behold, I have a weapon;
A better never did itself sustain
Upon a soldier's thigh. I have seen the day
That with this little arm and this good sword
I have made my way through more impediments
Than twenty times your stop. But O vain boast!
Who can control his fate? 'Tis not so now.
Be not afraid, though you do see me weaponed.
Here is my journey's end, here is my butt,
And very seamark of my utmost sail.
Do you go back dismayed? 'Tis a lost fear.
Man but a rush against Othello's breast,
And he retires. Where should Othello go?
Now, how dost thou look now? O ill-starred wench!
Pale as thy smock! When we shall meet at compt,
This look of thine will hurl my soul from heaven,
And fiends will snatch at it. Cold, cold, my girl,
Even like thy chastity!
O cursed, cursed slave! Whip me, ye devils,
From the possession of this heavenly sight!
Blow me about in winds! roast me in sulphur!
Wash me in steep-down gulfs of liquid fire!
O Desdemona, Desdemona dead!
O! O! O!

Shakespeare

(To preserve the euphony of the antepenultimate line, the reader is asked to bear in mind that in ancient Athens the vowel sounds of αι and ει were as different as those of night and day.)

LP. Πάρειμ᾽ ἀκούσας· τί δὲ θέλων τόσον βοᾷς;

ΟΘ. σκέψαι τόδ᾽, ὦνερ· ἔστι γὰρ δή μοι ξίφος,
οὗ φημ᾽ ἄμεινον οὐδέν᾽ ἄνδρα πώποτε
μηρῷ φορῆσαι, πρόσθε δ᾽ ἦν ποθ᾽ ἡνίκα
ξὺν φασγάνῳ τῷδ᾽ ἤ θ᾽ ὁρᾷς σμικρᾷ χερὶ
ἐναντίων κώλυμα πολλάκις τόσον
εἶχον διῶσαι· τί δὲ μάτην κομπῶ τάδε;
νῦν φροῦδ᾽ ἐκεῖνα, δυσπαλὴς γάρ τοι πότμος.
μηδὲν φοβηθῇς φάσγανον τόδ᾽ εἰσορῶν,
ὡς τῇδ᾽ ἄρ᾽ ἦν μοι τέρμα, τῇδ᾽ ὁδοῦ πέρας
πανύστατός τε ναυτίλου πρῴρας λιμήν.
χωρεῖς δεδοικώς; ἤ κενὸν τρέφεις φόβον·
ἅπαξ γὰρ ἤν τις τῷδ᾽ ἐφορμήσῃ κάρα
εἴκοιμ᾽ ἂν εὐθύς· ποῖ γὰρ ἔστι καὶ μολεῖν;
    ἰὼ κόρη δύστηνος, ὡς ὠχρὰν ἄρα,
πέπλοις συνῳδόν, νῦν ἔχεις παρηίδα.
εὖτ᾽ ἄν κρίταισι τοῖς ἐκεῖ στῶμεν πάρα,
ψυχῆς φανεῖται τῆς ἐμῆς κατήγορος
τοῦτ᾽ ἀβλαβὲς πρόσωπον, ὥστε μ᾽ ἐκπεσεῖν
Ἐρινύων ἅρπασμα. φεῦ ψυχρὸν δέμας,
ἁγνῶν γ᾽ ἐκείνων προσφερὲς σέθεν φρενῶν.
τὸν τρὶς δὲ τόνδ᾽ ἀραῖον—εἶ᾽, ἀλάστορες,
μάστιξί μ᾽ ἐξελαύνετ᾽, ἔνθα μήποτε
ὄψιν μάκαιραν τήνδ᾽ ἔτ᾽ ἔσται μοι βλέπειν.
πῶς οὔ με λάβρων διὰ πνοῶν διώκετε;
πῶς οὐχὶ θείῳ δείρετ᾽, ἤ δίναις ὕπο
στροβεῖτέ μ᾽ αἰπειναῖσι πυριφλέκτων ῥοῶν;
ἃ ἅ.
ὦ τῶν ἁπασῶν τιμιώτατον κάρα,
σὺ δή, σύ μοι τέθνηκας; ὦ τάλας ἐγώ.

My Epitaph

Ἔι τι μέλει, Μακρίδης Μακρίδου γόνος ἐνθάδε κεῖμαι,
  μέσσα δὲ γῆς Ἀγγλων ναῖον ἔτ' ὢν πεδία·
ἐλπομένῳ δὲ πρέπειν κιθάρει σφαίρᾳ τε κεκάσθαι
  κεῖνο διδοὺς βαιὸν Ζεὺς ἀνένευε τόδε.